THE WATKINS
TAROT
HANDBOOK

By the same author

Chakras: A Beginner's Guide
Meditation: A Beginner's Guide
Teach Yourself Meditation
New Perspectives: Chakras
Thorsons First Directions: Chakras
Teach Yourself Tarot
Dowsing: A Beginner's Guide
The Illustrated Guide to Tarot
The Little Book of Egyptian Wisdom
The Elements of The Chakras
101 Essential Tips: Basic Meditation
Daughter of the Goddess
The Aquarian Qabalah
Becoming a Garment of Isis

NAOMI OZANIEC

THE WATKINS
TAROT
HANDBOOK

*A Practical System
of Self-Discovery*

This edition published in 2022 by
Watkins, an imprint of Watkins Media Limited
Unit 11, Shepperton House
89-93 Shepperton Road
London
N1 3DF

enquiries@watkinspublishing.com

Originally published as *The Element Tarot Handbook* by Element Books Ltd Republished in
2002 as *Initiation into The Tarot* by Watkins Publishing

Interior design and typesetting by WestKey Ltd
Printed and bound in the United Kingdom by TJ Books Ltd

British Library Cataloguing in Publication data available

ISBN: 978-1-78678-667-8

www.watkinspublishing.com

If you would like to know more about becoming a companion in The House of Life,
visit: www.thehouseoflife.co.uk

Contents

List of Figures

To all the Good Companions in the House of Life

Acknowledgements

I would like to acknowledge all those whose work has helped to establish the Golden Path of Insight. I salute those who serve Wisdom by holding open its door for those who seek.

I would like to thank the following authors and publishers for permission to reproduce material from their publications.

Dolores Ashcroft-Nowicki, *The Shining Paths*, HarperCollins Publishers Ltd.

Paul Foster Case, *The True and Invisible Rosicrucian Order*, Samuel Weiser Inc., York Beach, Maine 03910–0612.

Gareth Knight, *A Practical Guide to Qabalistic Symbolism*, S. Weiser, York Beach, USA/Kahn and Averill, London. *Experience of the Inner Worlds*, S. Weiser, York Beach, USA/Kahn and Averill, London.

Stan Tenen and the Meru Foundation, PO Box 1938, San Anselmo, CA 94979, USA. Tel. (415) 4590487.

Strephon Kaplan Williams, *Jungian Senoi Dreamwork Manual*, Journey Press, Berkeley.

How to Use this Book

This book is intended to be interactive. So be prepared to become actively involved in your reading. The text invites you to undertake a journey of discovery and creativity. Here there are no fixed answers, only a multitude of possibilities.

The text is divided into two parts. Part 1 provides a series of exercises which are designed to inform the intellect, awaken intuition and precipitate insight. Work through them at your own pace and keep a record of your realisations in a journal. Do not rush through the chapters; here is an instance where speed is no virtue. Instead, as in creating a good wine, allow time for the fermentation and inner processes to take place.

Part II, The Serpent of Wisdom, offers a meditative text which can be used in a variety of ways. It may be read aloud with good effect, either as a whole or in parts. The text may be profitably incorporated into a Tarot workshop or used by a small group of Tarot enthusiasts as poetic invocation. The Serpent of Wisdom is intended to be a finale and culmination to your period of study, so do wait until you or your group have worked through the first part of the book.

Foreword

The Tarot has risen in popularity to become the singular form of Western divination, but the images of the Tarot have a deeper significance as icons for meditative reflection and as keys to unlock the creative potential of the mind. These sacred icons provide the means with which to navigate the hidden realms of the unconscious and with which to create links to the domain of higher consciousness. This is its initiatory function. The Tarot is both a psychic mirror and, as a multifaceted symbol system, it is also a spiritual powerhouse which can be entered and explored. Its archetypal images hold guidance, advice and insight but simultaneously these same images open the doors to the inner world of the psyche through the path of initiation.

The originator of the immensely popular Rider-Waite Tarot, Arthur Waite, understood this well. As a member of the Hermetic Order of the Golden Dawn, Waite designed the deck to encompass and portray a magical philosophy. In *The Pictorial Key to the Tarot* he wrote, 'The Tarot embodies symbolical presentations of universal ideas,' and, 'it is in this sense that they contain secret doctrine.' In other words Tarot images express a practical spiritual philosophy which will disclose its truths to the reflective mind in contemplative meditation. The initiatory path begins with this understanding. Divination, on the other hand is most often a commercial exchange where power remains in the hands of the Tarot reader. Initiation takes place in sacred space through an act of commitment not commerce. Divination guides but initiation empowers.

It should be clear that the sacred images of the Tarot serve a spiritual purpose. In common with the vast variety of worldwide spiritual icons, the sacred images of the Tarot serve to feed the reflective and contemplative instincts and as such have rightfully earned a place within the spiritual traditions of the west. The sacred icons of the Tarot form a key aspect of a Mystery School curriculum as doorways leading into the realm of the Ageless Wisdom. This is deeper gift of the Tarot.

Studying the Tarot is not a matter of memorising a collection of meanings but rather its sacred symbols are inwardly absorbed and digested to release a spiritual nutrition. This is not a single event but an ongoing, self-propelling process of dynamic change. In the fullness of time this process of forward momentum effects a cycle of death–renewal–rebirth, this is the essence of initiation. This is the way of the Tarot, this is the way of the Mystery School. Once we have awakened to Tarot's greater function, we, like the spiritual pilgrims of old, may also be stirred to go in search of initiation and discover its timeless yet totally personal importance on the road to Wisdom.

It is hoped that these few words may inspire you sufficiently to dare, to know, to will and to be silent in Wisdom's name.

Foreword to the
2022 Edition

This book was originally published in 2005 and the global outlook has changed a great deal in the intervening years. The current world crisis is unprecedented, its root causes are many but the unrelenting drive for material consumption has played its part in the construction of a value system quite divorced from reality. In contrast to the empty aspirations of a self-centred moral vacuum, the Tarot presents a spiritual philosophy, a philo-sophia, which means 'the love of wisdom'. The language of the Tarot is that of the symbol in many forms: numerical, mythical, elemental, zodiacal, alchemical and Hermetic. This is a code that feeds the imagination and restores the Ancient Wisdom to a much-needed place in the modern world. Here is a visual representation of the Western Esoteric Tradition, this eso-thodos: the inward path returns power to the individual through the initiatory journey which is the Journey of the Fool from innocence to illumination. Esoteric ideas are mistakenly assumed to be simply arcane or unworldly; on the contrary an esoteric perspective is applicable to the many choices to be made in life.

The images of the Tarot may rightly be understood as the Keys which unlock the hidden realms of the psyche with its rich storehouse of soul-infused creativity: these are the Keys of transformation. This alchemical process of personal transmutation is among the Four Intrinsic Characteristics of the esoteric philo-sophia. The remaining three qualities are also visibly present within the framework of Tarot: the Livingness of Nature is most palpably but not only demonstrated in the Icon of The Empress whose realm has been despoiled so cruelly. The notion that the visible universe is imbued with life-force opposes the utilitarian view that nature is merely a commodity at our disposal. The Law of Correspondences is a central Tarot theme and this idea suggests a connection between all parts of the universe. Finally the symbolic images of the Tarot feed the human imagination as intermediaries between the physical and spiritual realms.[1] This embedded esoteric philosophy will reward all time and energy spent in study and meditation with an abundant bounty of inspiration. These ideas of holistic existence - an engaged and harmonious relationship within nature and that of personal revelation made possible through the symbolic interface - together present a philosophical and practical alternative view of human purpose and aspiration. As the individual is transformed by a deep engagement with the spiritual themes of the Tarot, it is timely that Western society might benefit from its own esoteric tradition which has nourished the few in the past. Perhaps it is now possible for this rich feast to nourish the many into the future. This is the role of Tarot as initiator and the keys are in your hands.

---

[1] These are the Four Intrinsic Characteristics of Western Esotericism published by the scholar Antoine Faivre in 1992

PART ONE

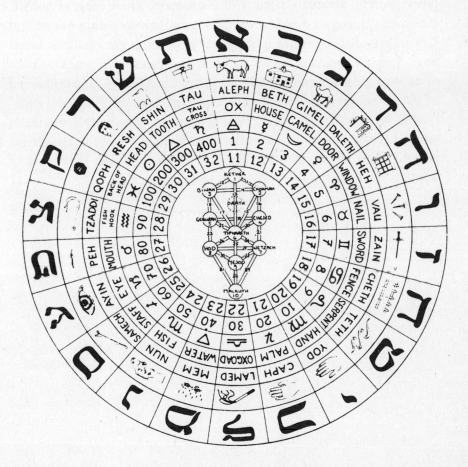

The Wheel of Correspondences
(from *The Shining Paths* by Dolores Ashcroft-Nowicki)

Introduction

To have the benefit of this wonderful invention, the Keys must be inside you. This means that you must be able to call up the images of any Key by a simple act of will. When you can do this, the Tarot will be part of your very flesh and blood, and it will begin to effect far reaching transformations in your thinking and thus in your living.
Paul Foster Case

The Tarot is too often associated with 'fortune telling'. This misrepresents the place, and diminishes the significance, of Tarot within the Western Tradition. The Tarot is primarily a vehicle for initiation. It is a means of divination only in a secondary role.

I was introduced to the Tarot in 1975. I was fascinated by the images. I took up my studies with relish. I worked with the cards both intellectually, struggling to recall correspondences and attributions, and intuitively by attempting to meditate on the images. I didn't feel I was having much success at either endeavour. I'm afraid I have to admit that I did most of my Tarot meditations in bed just before sleeping, not a recommended or indeed proper practice but it was truly the only space I could find for myself.

I had been working on the card of the Magician in the Rider–Waite deck. I followed the usual instructions, namely to create the images in the mind's eye. However on this occasion instead of the cardboard cut out, the Magician came to life in my mind's eye. He stood before me, crinkly hair as black as jet. His white inner garment was made of soft white linen. The serpent girdle glinted and shone. The circlet on his head was golden, unlike that on the card. He raised the rod aloft, his red tunic slipping slightly towards the shoulder as he did so. I was amazed. I have never stopped being amazed by the characters of the Tarot. This was my first initiation into the Tarot. It was not to be my last.

It is clear from my own experience that I had already begun to study Tarot some time before this particular experience. Up to that moment my studies had been purely intellectual. I had applied my memory to remember names that were new to me. I had struggled to understand concepts which were unfamiliar. I had endeavoured to learn long lists of correspondences. In that single meditation, my learning suddenly coalesced. I had passed from learning Tarot from the outside to understanding Tarot from within. I had undergone an *initiation*. I had passed with*in* the Tarot.

Initiation – The Beginning

Initiation is equivalent to a basic change in existential condition.
Mircea Eliade

Initiation simply means to begin. Life itself is a continuing process of initiation both biological and social. We are changed by the significant events of life as we move from childhood to adulthood, from adulthood to parenthood. These landmarks have profound changes on our outlook and philosophy. Indeed we expect to be changed by our experiences. If we are unable to respond to life's challenges, we simply fail to grow up and fail to shoulder the responsibilities of the adult world. The key word in this process is growth. We are certain of biological growth, we anticipate social growth, we forget spiritual growth. Our secular, materialist society has lost sight of spiritual values. We do not value the spiritual goal. We do not utilize initiation as a springboard into the spiritual life.

Initiation was once effected through ceremony which marked the difference between the old and the new in a definite and distinct manner. The Eleusinian Mysteries were the most prestigious and important initiatory ceremonies of the ancient world. Initiation may take place in many forms, through many triggers. Ceremonial initiation serves to reinforce a social, biological or spiritual landmark. Its theatrical nature has a purpose. All is designed to create a private inner experience, to bring out a personal realization. Initiation may be thought of as those experiences which precipitate a realization, a moment in which we learn a personal truth.

The images and ideas presented through the Tarot may also serve to initiate, to create change within us. For the themes depicted within the Major Arcana are exactly the same themes as those presented to all would-be initiates of all the ages. We are asked to consider the meaning of our life, to face the concept of death, to consider the idea of transformation. We are asked to examine our own value system. We may even discover that we have none. We can build a personal value system as we respond to fundamental questions. This is the meaning of initiation. We are not presented with a handed down dogma. We are not expected to defer to a spurious authority. We are instead taken *in* to ourselves. We are put in touch with the *inner* life of feelings and values. We are given the opportunity to grow as a spiritual being. Initiation is not an event but an ongoing process of events. Once begun the process is self-feeding and self-motivating. Initiation is the journey into self-discovery, the path of personal growth, the way to awaken.

My experiences are not unique or special. I have benefited immeasurably from my contact with the forces represented within the Tarot. I would like to share the processes with you. Welcome to the Tarot Initiation.

A Brief History of Tarot

Tarot in the form that we know it today dates back to the Middle Ages. The term *trionfi* was first used to describe the twenty-two cards of the Major Arcana. This was later replaced by the term *tarocchi* which was also used to describe both Major and Minor Arcana. Tarot is the French derivative of the Italian term.

The earliest pack originated in the mid-fifteenth century during a time of great interest in Hermetic philosophy and ideas. Marsilio Ficino, under the patronage of Cosimo de'Medici, had translated important Greek Hermetic works. The Visconti–Sforza *tarocchi* were made for the families of Visconti and Sforza. The images of the hand painted set were probably used as images for private meditation. It would have been in keeping with the newly-emerging spirit of the day.

With the development of woodblock printing Tarot became increasingly popular. It evolved into a Tarot game which did not decline in favour until about 1700. The Tarot has twin identities as both magical image and gaming device. The one does not preclude the success of the other. Its decline as a game, however, coincided with a renewed interest in its esoteric function. The instructions and descriptions for the game were finally dropped from *La Maison academique de jeux*, a popular gaming manual, in 1718. 1718 is the same year from which we can date the manufacture of the earliest Marseilles Tarot.

In the late eighteenth century, the esoteric import placed on the Tarot Trumps was given a boost in the writings of Court de Gebelin. In *Monde primitif* he wrote the following.

Imagine the surprise which the discovery of an Egyptian book would cause if we learned that a work of the ancient Egyptian still existed … This book does exist. This Egyptian book is all that remains of their superb libraries. It is even so common that not one scholar has condescended to bother with it since no one before us has ever suspected its illustrious origins. The book is composed of seventy-seven, even seventy-eight sheets or pictures divided into five classes, each showing things which are as varied as they are amusing and instructive. In a word this is the game of Tarot.[1]

He claimed unequivocal Egyptian roots for the Tarot. According to Gebelin, it was the surviving example of Ancient Wisdom, rendered into symbols by an arcane priesthood. He also claimed that the twenty-two Trumps corresponded to the twenty-two letters of the Hebrew alphabet. His ideas were enough to fire a French imagination already awakened to exotic Egyptian images by French explorers and expeditions. It was one of Napoleon's troops after all who had shot the nose from the Sphinx, that most enigmatic of all Egyptian symbols.

These ideas fuelled a French occult revival. It produced the usual occult gamut from fortune telling and notable, or indeed notorious, fortune tellers to a renewed interest in magical orders and occult symbols. One Etteilla, whose real name was Alliette, rose to prominence on the crest of this wave. He produced the first 'rectified' Tarot pack. He modified current images, theoretically restoring them to a former arcane meaning. A more substantive esoteric contribution was made by Alphonse Louis Constant (1810–75) who wrote under the pen name of Eliphas Levi. He wanted to rectify the Marseilles Tarot but failed to achieve his ambition.

In 1888 two important magical orders were formed. The Cabalistic Order of the Rosy Cross was founded in France by Marquis Stanislaus de Guaita (1861–97), an admirer of Levi's work. The Hermetic Order of the Golden Dawn was founded in England. Both groups contributed significantly to the development and magical use of Tarot. Both groups produced their own suitably rectified Tarot. Guaita, in conjunction with Oswald Wirth, produced a limited edition of 350 copies in 1889 fulfilling Levi's intention. The Golden Dawn gave rise to several Tarot versions. A.E. Waite, who went on to found the Fellowship of the True Rosy Cross, devised the pack now called the Rider–Waite Tarot. It has remained an esoteric standard to this day. He discussed the production of the deck in his autobiography, *Shadows of Life and Thought*. He called the project 'a delightful experiment' and described Pamela Coleman Smith as 'a most imaginative and abnormally psychic artist'.[2] Aleister Crowley, another G.D. member, produced his idiosyncratic Tarot, *The Book of Thoth*, in conjunction with the artist, Freida Harris. The project was begun in 1938 and not completed until 1943. Freida Harris wrote of their collaboration:

> We tottered along for five years wrestling with the accumulated mass of tradition emanating from sources such as Freemasons, Alchemists, Rosicrucians, Kabbalists, Geometricians, Gematricians, Mathematicians, Symbolists, Philologists, Buddhists, Togas, Psychoanalysts, Astrologers even Heraldry, all of whom have left traces on the symbols employed.[3]

Paul Foster Case, an American member of the Golden Dawn, who went on to found B.O.T.A., the Builders of the Adytum, also devised his own set, a slightly modified version of the Rider–Waite imagery. It was not until 1977 that an authentic version of the original Golden Dawn group Tarot emerged through the collaborative work of Israel Regardie and Robert Wang. More recently a contemporary Mystery School, The Servants of the Light, have produced a Tarot pack designed by Jo Gill. Another contemporary occultist, Gareth Knight, has produced his own pack.

Tarot continues to take new and sometimes extraordinary forms. Tarot cards have been cast in Egyptian, Arthurian, even traditional Guatemalan, mode. The images have been represented entirely through astrological symbols, through sea shells and marine life. Surrealist artists have delighted in the otherworld quality of the Tarot. The Scottish artist Fergus Hall produced the pack which featured in the James Bond film 'Live and Let Die'. The unequalled Salvador Dali also produced a Tarot pack.

It seems that the Tarot offers inexhaustible inspiration. Doubtless other packs are still in the wings just waiting to make a debut. We have Spanish Tarot, Aquarian Tarot, British Tarot and even Tarot for Lovers.

Let us now explore the endless appeal of Tarot. Let us now begin to examine the Tarot in more depth.

The Structure of Tarot

THE MAJOR ARCANA

The Major Arcana consists of twenty-two cards. These represent the archetypal forces within our lives. They represent and depict life forces that underpin human life. Here we find the search for transcendence, the pull of matter, the power of love, the quality of wisdom. Here we find beginnings and endings, birth, death and resurrection. Here is a philosophy enshrined in pictures. Surprisingly enough we find the religious theme of redemptive sacrifice. We also encounter the central reality of the ancient mystery religions, namely initiation and transformation. Indeed the cards of the Major Arcana have the power both to initiate and transform.

The Major Arcana cards are also known as Trumps, a term derived from the Latin *trionfi*. The term Arcana is derived from the Latin *arcanum* meaning a mystery or a secret. Perhaps this provides us with a clue, the twenty-two major cards can be regarded as triumphal secrets or mysteries.

Each Trump is represented by a primary image, a name, a title, a Hebrew letter, a number, and an astrological correspondence.

Each of these symbolic attributions adds to our understanding of the Trump. The twenty-two Trumps can be arranged in three groups of seven. This gives us our first key with which to examine the Tarot. The first row represents powers or potencies, the second row represents laws or agencies, the third row represents conditions or effects.

THE MINOR ARCANA

The Minor Arcana consists of fifty-six pip cards subdivided into four elemental suits. The original emblems were Swords (*spade*), Wands (*bastoni*), Cups (*coppe*) and Coins (*denari*). The symbols represent the elements in the following way:

Earth	Discs, Coins, or Pantacles
Air	Swords
Water	Cups
Fire	Wands, Rods, Batons

The suits contain cards which run from ace to ten with four court cards, King, Queen, Knight and Page. The Knight and Page are sometimes referred to as the Prince and Princess. These cards carry less weight than the Major Arcana. They are used in conjunction with the Major Arcana when divination is appropriate.

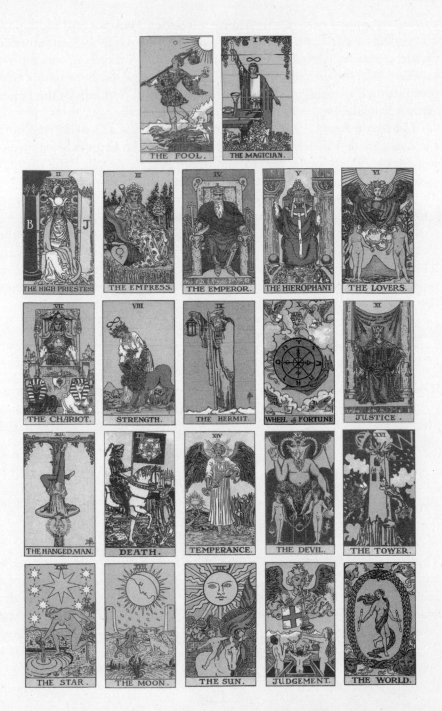

Fig. 1. The Twenty-two cards of the Major Arcana

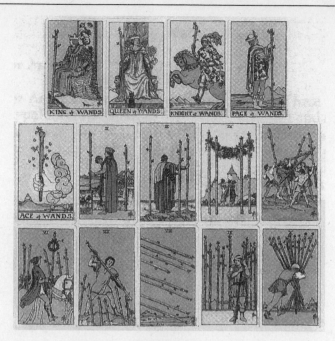

(a) Wands

(b) Cups

Fig. 2. The Fifty-six cards of the Minor Arcana

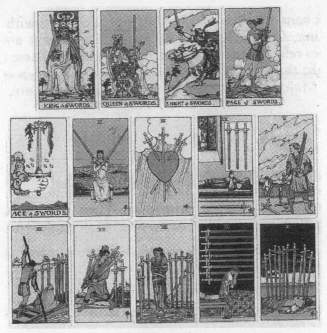

(c) Swords

(d) Pentacles

Approaching The Tarot

In the beginning understanding the Tarot may seem daunting. Quite simply do not try to commit lists of meanings to memory. The Tarot is constructed upon certain principles. When these basic principles have been grasped there will be no need to struggle with meanings.

PRINCIPLES

1. Each card is constructed upon a constellation of symbols.
2. The meaning of the card derives directly from the symbols.
3. The symbols have to be worked upon directly through reason and indirectly through the intuition.

Let us now embark upon our exploration into Tarot. It has been called The Royal Road and The Journey of the Fool. Let us be prepared to make discoveries and unearth hidden treasure.

Like the Fool you are about to step over the precipice of your existing belief system. Are you ready to take a quantum leap in consciousness?

Fig. 3. The Fool Takes the First Step on the Journey

CHAPTER ONE

Names and Titles

The most important use of Tarot is to evoke thought.
Paul Foster Case

When we are introduced to someone at a party, we normally make an effort to remember their name. Let me introduce you to the characters of the Tarot in exactly the same way. At this gathering we will find:

The Fool	Justice
The Magician	The Hanged Man
The High Priestess	Death
The Empress	Temperance
The Emperor	The Devil
The Hierophant	The Tower
The Lovers	The Star
The Charioteer	The Moon
Strength	The Sun
The Hermit	Judgement
The Wheel	The World

You may be surprised to discover just how much you can learn about these characters by just knowing their names. Let us meet and mingle with the Tarot cast.

In Fool's costume a youth sets out to amuse. A Magician performs tricks at a table. You wonder if he has any real magical powers. On a great chair a woman sits giving advice to a small group who listen keenly to every word. You wonder what the High Priestess is saying. The Empress and Emperor are clearly rulers of some kind. There is the priest known by a more ancient title, the Hierophant. Over there you see the two Lovers, clearly besotted with one another. Into the room strides the Charioteer, hot from the ride.

A beautiful woman in a white dress plays with a lion as if it were a kitten. You are amazed by her Strength. A man walks alone wrapped in his

Fig. 4. Collage of Tarot Characters

thoughts holding a dark cloak tightly about him. He is clearly the Hermit. A man sings, 'the times they are a changing'. He wears a bright T-shirt. On the front is a Wheel. A Judge in wig and red robes sits behind his bench. A man hangs upside down from a beam, tied by a rope around his foot. You think he is probably quite mad. You wonder for a moment if this is some kind of punishment administered by the Judge yet the Hanged Man has a serene and calm expression. A hooded man wielding a scythe weaves in and out of the assembly. Everyone steps aside from him but Death knows all their names. In another part of the room a figure on a soapbox is trying to persuade a small group about the dangers of excess. You are reminded of the Temperance League.

In another part of the room a man has evidently just persuaded a young couple to purchase something. They are signing the contract. There is something about him that you do not trust. He has a glint in his eye that reminds you of depictions of the Devil. You wonder what the young couple have agreed to. Another man carrying architectural implements is discussing the need for solid foundations. You overhear him say, 'the higher the tower, the deeper the foundations or else'. An astronomer is discussing the life cycle of a Star and the wonders of the physical universe. A young woman, Selene by name, is having a private conversation with her brother named Sol. They are as different as chalk and cheese. She is quiet, pale and somewhat mysterious. He is extravagant, loud and scintillating. A man paces the floor bearing a sandwich board with the words, 'Awake Now, Judgement is Nigh'. Someone projects pictures onto the far wall. You see the World against the background of space. This is your home planet Earth.

Now you have met all the Tarot characters. Let us see what else they have to tell us about themselves.

EXERCISE 1

Take the names of the Tarot Trumps in turn. Write down all the free associations that spring to mind.

For example, **Star** bright, shining, heavenly light, cosmic, something beautiful out of reach, enigmatic.

Moon waxes and wanes, changes shape, pulls up the tides, causes other fluids to ebb and flow, connected with menstruation, lunar goddesses.

EXERCISE 2

Take the names of the Tarot Trumps in turn. Write down all the associated images, settings and symbols that you would choose to depict the function of each character.

For example, **High Priestess** a woman, air of mystery and ancient religion, perhaps in or near a temple.

The World different landscapes, the planet earth, the solar system, mother earth.

In the long history of the Tarot, the Trumps have been known by various names. The Magician has in the past been called the Juggler, the Mountebank, the Wizard and the Minstrel.

Trump III now known as the Empress was once called the Papess. This referred to a circulating medieval tale of the female Pope Joan whose real identity was discovered when she died in childbirth in mid procession.

The Trump now known as the Emperor has also been called the Grandfather.

The Trump known now as the Lovers has been called Eros, Venus and Marriage. The Hermit has been called the Sage, the Aged Man and Father Time.

The Wheel of Fortune has been called Chance and Rota. Death has been called the Skeleton. The final card of the series, Tarot Trump XXI, the World, is now more often called the Universe. Exploration of space has resulted in an expansion of consciousness.

As we can see these name changes are quite superficial. The essential nature of each character remains much the same.

Names, Esoteric and Exoteric

The exoteric name may be likened to a personal surname. It is the name by which we are commonly known. By contrast when we get to know someone well, we share first names. We do not share our Christian name with just anyone. The esoteric title like a personal name is a great deal more revealing. The lesser-known name is considered to be the esoteric title. When we learn the esoteric titles of the Tarot characters, we will learn a great deal more about them. The following esoteric titles which originated with Crowley have a strong Qabalistic resonance.

TABLE 1
TAROT NAMES AND TITLES

Exoteric Name	Esoteric Title
The Fool	The Spirit of Aethyr
The Magician	The Magus of Power
The High Priestess	Priestess of the Silver Star
The Empress	Daughter of the Mighty Ones
The Emperor	Son of the Morning, Chief among the Mighty
The Hierophant	Magus of the Eternal
The Lovers	Children of the Voice, Oracle of the Mighty Gods
The Chariot	Child of the Powers of the Waters, Lord of the Triumph of Light
Strength	Daughter of the Flaming Sword, Leader of the Lion
The Hermit	Prophet of the Eternal, Magus of the Voice of Power
The Wheel	Lord of the Forces of Life
Justice	Daughter of the Lords of Truth, Ruler of the Balance
The Hanged Man	Spirit of the Mighty Waters
Death	Child of the Great Transformers, Lord of the Gates of Death
Temperance	Daughter of the Reconcilers, Bringer Forth of Life
The Devil	Lord of the Gates of Matter, Child of the Forces of Time
The Tower	Lord of the Hosts of the Mighty
The Star	Daughter of the Firmament, Dweller between the Waters
The Moon	Ruler of Flux and Reflux
The Sun	Lord of the Fire of the World
Judgement	Spirit of Primal Fire
The World	Great One of the Night of Time

The difference between an exoteric and esoteric understanding of Tarot is immense. The former is concerned with remembering names, the latter grows from understanding the significance of both names and titles. The first is related to appearance, the second to structure. The one seeks familiarity, the other seeks transformation.

EXERCISE 3

Compare the exoteric name with the esoteric titles.
For example, **The Devil – Lord of the Gates of Matter, Child of the Forces of Time.**

The Devil has an exclusively negative persona. However, the esoteric titles for this Trump prompts us to consider the Saturnian limitations represented by both matter and time which are among the two great mysteries of existence.

The Minor Arcana

Crowley also attributed titles to the Minor Arcana. These evocative titles express the essential nature of the pip cards more powerfully than mere description. For instance 'Two Wands', conveys little, yet its title 'Dominion' instantly tells us something more. The Aces are described as the 'Roots of the Powers' of each suit. We may think of them as the seeds of the elements. In the Aces, we find elemental beginnings. In the Tens we find the final concretion of the elemental powers. We find a gradual descent of energy from the purest spiritual form represented by the Ace to the most dense form represented by the Ten in accordance with the concept of Maya.

The Suit of Wands
1. The Root of the Powers of Fire
2. Dominion
3. Virtue
4. Completion
5. Strife
6. Victory
7. Valour
8. Swiftness
9. Strength
10. Oppression

The Suit of Cups
1. The Root of the Powers of Water
2. Love
3. Abundance
4. Luxury
5. Disappointment
6. Pleasure
7. Debauch
8. Indolence
9. Happiness
10. Satiety

The Suit of Swords
1. The Root of the Powers of Air
2. Peace
3. Sorrow
4. Truce
5. Defeat
6. Science
7. Futility
8. Interference
9. Cruelty
10. Ruin

The Suit of Discs

1. The Root of the Powers of Earth
2. Change
3. Work
4. Power
5. Worry

6. Success
7. Failure
8. Prudence
9. Gain
10. Wealth

EXERCISE 4

Take the names of the Minor Arcana in turn. Write down all the free associations that spring to mind.

For example, **Work** – labour, struggle, effort.

Ruin – disaster, failure, catastrophe, loss, upheaval, trauma.

Tarot Trumps, Titles and Initiation

*To succeed, we need undertake but one work at first – that which
the Sphinx depicts to us: moral and intellectual preparations.
But only the man who seriously undertakes them can know what
immense and persevering efforts they exact. May this rough glimpse
of them inspire the reader with the desire and the courage to
devote himself to them with all the ardour of Hope.*
F. Ch. Barlet

Crowley was not alone in attributing new titles to the Trumps. In France in 1863, Jean Baptiste Pitois writing under the name of Paul Christian produced *L'Homme rouge des Tuileries*. It took the form of an old manuscript written by a monk supposedly copied from seventy-eight gold leaves from an Egyptian temple in Memphis. The Samaritan Oracle is clearly another name for the Tarot. Its titles are as follows:

I	The Magus
II	The Gate of the Sanctuary
III	Isis Urania
IV	The Cubic Stone
V	Master of the Mysteries of Arcana
VI	The Two Roads
VII	The Chariot of Osiris
VIII	Themis, The Scales and the Blade

IX   The Veiled Lamp
X   The Sphinx
XI   The Muzzled or Tamed Lion
XII   The Sacrifice or the Great Work
XIII   The Skeleton, Reaper or Scythe
XIV   The Two Urns or Genius of the Sun
XV   Typhon, The Electrical Whirlwind
XVI   The Beheaded or Lightning Struck Tower
XVII   The Star of the Magi
XVIII   Twilight
XIX   The Resplendent Light
XX   The Awakening of the Dead
0   The Crocodile
XXI   The Crown of the Magi

Christian placed the Fool between XX and XXI following the lead given by Eliphas Levi. In 1870 Christian published *A History of Magic* which contained an initiatory sequence in an Egyptian setting. This theme reappeared in the French tradition. It resurfaced in *The Tarot of the Bohemians* by Papus as a supplementary chapter by Barlet. In his chapter, The Initiative Tarot, the Tarot Trumps are used to define the sequence of initiation. 'We will describe the twelve hours or phases of initiation'.[1] The first ten Trumps are seen as descriptions of the Path of Involution. The remaining ten Trumps excluding the Fool are used to describe the successive phases of the Path of Evolution. According to Barlet the initiation took place within the Sphinx. The neophyte descended between its paws into the tunnel which led to the sanctuary.

This first hour was symbolized by Trump X, the Sphinx. Each element of the Sphinx addresses the neophyte in turn. The human head speaks to the neophyte saying, 'First acquire that knowledge which shows the goal and lights the way to it.' The bull aspect of the Sphinx represented in the thighs speaks accordingly. 'Be strong and patient in thy work.' The leonine aspect of the Sphinx represented by the paws addresses the neophyte, 'Thou must brave all and defend thyself against every inferior force.' Finally the eagle aspect of the Sphinx represented by the wings speaks too, 'Thou must will to raise thyself towards the transcendent regions which thy soul already approaches.'

The first hour passes. The neophyte descends three further steps symbolized by Trumps XI, XII and XIII Strength, the Great Work and the Reaper which is Death. The fifth hour is represented by Trump XIV, the Two Urns. The sixth hour is represented by the figure of Typhon. At this point the neophyte passes into higher regions by crossing what is described as 'the dragon of the threshold'. This must surely be 'the dweller on the threshold'.

The seventh hour is represented by the Lightning Struck Tower. The eighth hour is represented by the Star. The ninth hour is represented by Twilight. The tenth hour is represented by the Resplendent Light. The eleventh hour is represented by the Awakening of the Dead. Finally the twelfth hour is represented by the Crown of the Magi.

The initiatory schema is interesting. It is historically fanciful. Initiations, however, do not require historical authenticity to be successful, a fact not

0.—Preliminary studies and tests.		Arcanum X.	1st hour
I.—Transcendental study of the *Visible World.*			
Inferior Manifestations :			
1. Preliminary study of Force.	(*Magnetism*)	Arcanum XI.	2nd hour
2. Application to the inert world.	(*Alchemy*)	Arcanum XII.	3rd hour
3. Application to the animate elementary world.	(*Necromancy*) (*Magic*)	Arcanum XIII. (DEATH)	4th hour
Transitory phase :			
1. View of the superior forces.		Arcanum XIV.	5th hour
2. Entrance into the ultra-terrestrial world.	(*Ecstasy*)	Arcanum XV. (TYPHON)	6th hour
THE DRAGON OF THE THRESHOLD !			
Higher regions :			
1. Application of the higher forces to the terrestrial life.	(*Therapeutics*)	Arcanum XVI.	7th hour
2. The forces in the solar system.	(*Astrology*)	Arcanum XVII.	8th hour
3. The forces of the whole Universe.		Arcanum XVIII.	9th hour
II.—Study of the *Intelligible World.* On the borders of the Infinite.		Arcanum XIX.	10th hour
III.—Study of the *Divine World.* Divine hierarchies		Arcanum XX.	11th hour
Nirvana !		Arcanum XXII.	12th hour

*Fig. 5. Initiatory Schema given by F. Ch. Barlet in
The Tarot of the Bohemians by Papus*

appreciated by critical minds. Authentic Egyptian cult practice was commonly divided into hourly watches each with its characteristic gods and cultic correspondences. The magical orders which sprang up around the turn of the century both in England and in France systematized these very principles employing the creative imagination to travel constructively in the mind to encounter pre-established symbolic realities.

Apart from the names and titles of the Trumps, the Tarot makes subtle use of certain names, most especially the Tetragrammaton, the Holy Name of God.

The Holy Name of God

It may come as a surprise to discover that the Tarot resonates to the Tetragrammaton, The Holy Name of God. It is an idea we will meet again as we continue our journey through the Tarot. Traditionally the name of God was considered too holy to pronounce. The name IHVH (pronounced Eh-ah-oo-eh) was rendered as JHVH (יהוה) and as Jehovah by early gentile scholars unfamiliar with the finer points of the Hebrew. In common with hieroglyphics, individual Hebrew letters also carry symbolic meanings. Words thereby have an additional meaning over and above simple spelling. When we look at YHVH, we find the letters Yod, Heh, Vau and the final Heh. Analysis of these letters yields the following:

י	**Yod**	signifies the open hand of a man. It implies power, direction, skill and dexterity. The open hand symbolises beneficence a sign of the Supreme Spirit.
ה	**Heh**	signifies a window which permits light and two way vision.
ו	**Vau**	signifies a nail which joins things together creating union. Grammatically it is used like *and* to join phrases together. It is very close in concept to the Sanskrit 'yoga' which means union.
ה	**Heh**	represents the end result of the process.

We can already see how this constellation of ideas gels to create a powerful image. The beneficent active, open hand of deity like a window in a darkened room establishes both light and two way vision.

The Tetragrammaton is a vital key if we are to understand the internal structure of the Tarot. We should regard the Tetragrammaton as a formula

Fig. 6. The Tetragrammaton

which signifies the four elements, the four worlds of the Qabalah, the four suits and the four court cards. In order to understand these relationships we need to explore the full symbolic range of ideas and images attributed to each individual letter.

TABLE 2
THE TETRAGRAMMATON AND THE ELEMENTS

Yod	The Element of Fire	Primal Emanation
Heh	The Element of Water	Transmission
Vau	The Element of Air	Stabilization
Heh	The Element of Earth	Consolidation

EXERCISE 5

What qualities do you associate with the Element of Fire?
For example, dynamic, explosive, the Big Bang, dangerous, cosmic, the sun.
What qualities do you associate with the Element of Water?
For example, fluid, reflective without form, life-giving, cleansing.
What qualities do you associate with the Element of Air?
For example, invisible, all pervading, formless.
What qualities do you associate with the Element of Earth?
For example, inertia, a myriad of forms.

The Court Cards are also assigned to the four elements. The King and the Prince or Knight, the dynamic male roles, are assigned to the elements of Fire and Air. The Queen and the Princess, the receptive female roles, are assigned to the elements of Water and Earth.

TABLE 3
THE TETRAGRAMMATON AND THE COURT CARDS

Yod	The Kings	The Powers of Dynamic Emanation
Heh	The Queens	The Powers of Transmission
Vau	The Princes or Knights	The Powers of Stabilization
Heh	The Princesses or Pages	The Powers of Consolidation

EXERCISE 6

What qualities of being do you associate with the role of King, Queen, Prince and Princess?

We have already seen how the four elements are attributed to the Tetragrammaton. Additionally each suit is also assigned to one of the four letters. This attribution should add to our understanding of the nature of the elements and the qualities ascribed to each of the four suits.

The Suit of Wands is considered to be fiery, primal spirit, outgoing and dynamic. Its symbol, the rod or staff, is that which gives support. It is the backbone which takes shape first. The Suit of Cups is clearly watery in quality. The cup provides form. It is a container for that which has no shape of its own. As a woman's body holds the living waters in pregnancy, so the Suit of Cups is clearly feminine. The Suit of Swords is likened to an airy quality. The sword is that which divides. It is wielded through the air. It cleaves, divides and separates. The sword is a man's weapon. The remaining suit is symbolized by a variety of images each representing an aspect of physical manifestation. The Suit of Coins, Pantacles or Discs is clearly earthy in quality. The coin symbolizes the man-made world of commerce and financial exchange. The Pantacle, a circular disc inscribed with a pentacle, represents the sacred appearance of matter. The disc likewise represents form. Here are images of Maya, the world of appearance directly and intimately descended from the world of spirit.

TABLE 4
THE TETRAGRAMMATON AND THE
TAROT SUITS

Yod	The Suit of Rods	Fiery
Heh	The Suit of Cups	Watery
Vau	The Suit of Swords	Airy
Heh	The Suit of Discs, Pantacles	Earthy

EXERCISE 7

What qualities and characteristics do you associate with Yod?

For example, the dynamic impulse to life, the first explosion.

What qualities do you associate with Heh?

For example, the developing seed, the emergence of life.

What qualities do you associate with Vau?

For example, the conjunction of opposites, union.

What qualities do you associate with Heh final?

For example, the final appearance of form, concretion, matter.

EXERCISE 8

Draw a circle and place each letter of the Tetragrammaton in one quarter. What do you discover about the Tetragrammaton as a unity?

CHAPTER TWO

Symbols and Images

The Tarot is a book, disguised as a pack of cards.
Paul Foster Case

We think in words but understand through symbols. Words have a precision and narrow application which is necessary in the right context. It is a mistake to believe that word-dominated thinking is the right tool for every situation. When we confront fundamental issues of belief and comprehension we need a depth and breadth of thought. We use a symbol. A symbol permits mental exploration, unlimited association of ideas and free flow of the emotions. Every symbol permits an unlimited process of association to take place. Oswald Wirth quite rightly said: 'A symbol can always be studied from an infinite number of points of view, and each thinker has the right to discover in the symbol a new meaning corresponding to the logic of his own conceptions.'[1] We are so used to thinking of our responses only in terms of 'right' and 'wrong'. We too need to make a mental leap. A symbol frees us from the tyranny of the mental straitjacket. Our response to the symbol is all that we need.

It is no coincidence that all spiritual traditions also include a rich storytelling vein. Jesus conveyed his teachings in parable form. The storytelling vehicle conveys meaning through symbols. When Jesus spoke of vineyards, barren ground, seeds and corn, he was not speaking literally but metaphorically. Jesus made a clear distinction between the vehicle of revelation given to the disciples and the vehicle of revelation appropriate to all others. To the disciples, he said: 'To you the secret of the kingdom of God has been given; but to those who are outside everything comes by way of parables.' (Mark 4: 11–12)

We can regard the Tarot Trumps as stories or parables rendered into visual form. Together the Trumps create a vehicle for a personal revelation. Whether we are open to the revelation contained here is another issue. We may be like 'those who receive the seed on rocky ground'. We may simply lack the staying-power. We may 'receive the seed among thistles'. We will be turned away from the goal by the 'false glamour of wealth and all kinds

of evil desire'. On the other hand we may 'receive the seed in good soil'
and 'bear fruit thirtyfold, sixtyfold, or a hundredfold'.

EXERCISE 9

Make up a short story for each of the Tarot Trumps.

For example, A man fell into a deep sleep and in it he experienced
a great vision. It seemed to him that he saw a huge wheel filling the
sky. And within the wheel was another wheel. As he watched the
wheels began to turn, one within another.

As he looked, it seemed to him that figures began to form from
within the clouds. He saw a bull and a man, an eagle and a lion. And
each figure carried a book which was opened before the man.
And close to the wheel the man saw a serpent undulating through
space. As his eyes became adjusted to the brightness of the vision, he
saw that the wheel carried a strange being upon its rim. Its body was
human but its head was that of an animal. And the man wondered
how this animal-headed being was served by the wheel. The man
saw that a huge Sphinx armed with a sword sat at the top of the
wheel. And the lights began to fade. The man awoke and wondered
what he had seen. But he knew that he had seen the Wheel.

Let us begin to explore the symbolism of the Tarot. A symbol has the
power to lead the mind on an unlimited trail of associations. This is the
strength of symbolic imagery. It opens up the deeper recesses of understanding. The Tarot is an interconnected symbol system. Tarot combines
images, piling meaning upon meaning with the precision of a military
manoeuvre. To unlock the meaning hidden in the symbolic forms we
need to apply the right key.

We need to approach the Tarot as we might approach a puzzle or code.
We need to become aware of cross references and subtle clues. We need to
look out for symbols within symbols and even false trails designed to trap
the unwary. We will not find explicit meaning upon the surface, but if we
are patient we will find it beneath the surface. We need to approach all the
symbols both through the intellect and insight. Intellectual understanding
comes from study, insight comes from meditation.

Tarot symbols can be examined from within certain categories. When
we have understood the relevant symbols in any particular context, we have
to be prepared to look at the same symbols in another context. Analysis
must never become a prison, it is only a tool. Let us now turn specifically to
the symbols of the Tarot.

Mythological Figures

The Tarot draws heavily upon familiar mythology and introduces us to some figures who may be less instantly recognizable. Even in the age of computer games, children still fortunately are acquainted with the stories and deeds of the Greek gods and goddesses. Children are still told the story of Demeter and Persephone. Demeter represents Mother Nature. When she grieves and searches for her lost daughter, the earth falls into ruin and everything dies. When we see the Empress we see Demeter, the Earth Mother.

Demeter was connected with both the fertility of women and the land. In an annual three-day festival, the Thesmophoria, women gathered to descend into caverns. They carried offerings into the earth to symbolize the cycle of renewal. We have no celebrations with which we honour the Earth.

EXERCISE 10

Find out all you can about the goddess Demeter.

By contrast the naked figure shown in Tarot Trump XVII represents the heavens. She is Nuit or Nut. She is usually depicted in the form of a woman bearing a vase of water upon her head. The vase carries the phonetic value Nu indicating both her name and her nature. She sometimes appears in the likeness of the goddess Hathor. She stands within a sycamore tree and pours water from a vase. The resemblance between the image of Tarot Trump XVII, commonly called the Star and the mythology assigned to Nut is very striking. It is also curious to note that the hieroglyphic signs for her name contains the sign ᴍᴧ, denoting the sound N. This same sign denoted water to the Egyptians and now the same sign is used twice to represent the sign of Aquarius also known as the Water Bearer. The esoteric title given to this Tarot Trump is Daughter of the Firmament, Dweller Between the Waters.

EXERCISE 11

Find out all you can about the Egyptian goddess Nut.

Tarot Trump XVII appears to show us only one mythological figure, yet in the true spirit of treasure trail, it provides hints which take us on to another clue. In the background we see a bird perched in a tree. This is an ibis bird, the long curved bill is unmistakable. The ibis bird is sacred to Thoth, the Egyptian god of Wisdom.

The long hooked beak of the ibis is not unlike the scribe's writing implement. Furthermore the ibis feeds by dipping its bill beneath the waters. It stands patiently waiting and watching below the surface. This clue should remind us that Tarot has been called the Book of Thoth. In other words, the Tarot may be regarded as the book of Wisdom. If we wish to be fed by it we must be like the ibis, patient ever watchful, ready to plunge beneath the surface at the appropriate moment.

EXERCISE 12

Find out what you can about the Egyptian god Thoth.

The goddess Nut is also connected to another figure, namely Isis. According-ing to some stories Nut was the mother of Isis. When Nut saw her child she exclaimed, 'As (that is, behold), I have become thy mother.'[2] This thereby became the origin of the name, Ast or Isis. The goddess Isis was a key figure in the Egyptian Mysteries. She was called the 'great goddess'. Her sign was the throne. She was the great empowerer, the king maker. Her sign in the heavens was the star Sirius, the brightest star of the skies. When we see Tarot Trump II commonly called the High Priestess, we see the servant of Isis, her earthly representative, Priestess of the Silver Star.

EXERCISE 13

Find out what you can about the Egyptian goddess Isis.

The two figures seen on Tarot Trump VI, the Lovers, are easily identified as Adam and Eve, the first man and woman, archetypal male and female. This particular mythology takes us back to the Garden of Eden, the serpent and the Tree of the Knowledge of Good and Evil,

According to the myth when the pair were exiled from the Garden, an angel with a flaming sword barred their return. We also see an angelic force in Tarot Trump VI. We do not see a flaming sword. However it is curious to note that the Hebrew letter assigned to this trump is Zain, meaning a sword!

Angels

The Tarot, like the Bible, contains several angelic figures. Angels tradition-
ally act as divine messengers. The angel Gabriel acted as enunciator to
Mary. The Koran was traditionally received from Gabriel too. The name
Gabriel means, 'The Strong One of God'. According to tradition, Qabalah
was also received through angelic revelation. The angelic presence repre-
sents a higher form of consciousness originating outside the human mind.
We find that angels are represented on Trump VI, Trump XX and Trump
XIV.

If we are to understand the full meanings of these particular Trumps,
we need to become familiar with the functions traditionally assigned to
certain angels. Qabalah recognizes a complex hierarchy of angelic beings
and attributes.

The four elements are also associated with a different angelic presence.

TABLE 5
THE ARCHANGELS AND THE ELEMENTS

The Element of Earth	Uriel
The Element of Air	Raphael
The Element of Fire	Michael
The Element of Water	Gabriel

Identifying the angels depicted on the three Trumps is not as straightforward as this basic table of correspondences might indicate. Different
authorities prefer different interpretations. This is an object lesson in itself.
The flexibility presented through a symbol system does not preclude various interpretations. For instance, according to William Gray, respected
twentieth-century Qabalist, the angel depicted on Trump XX is Gabriel
whose sign is the Horn of Annunciation and the element of Water. On the
other hand, it is more common to see this force as being Michael, archangel of Fire. This corresponds to the esoteric title of this Trump, the
Spirit of Primal Fire. Gareth Knight treats the angel depicted on Trump
XIV as Raphael. Paul Foster Case, another celebrated twentieth-century
teacher, regards this angel as Michael. Do not let these apparent contra-
dictions confuse you. You need to come to your own understanding and
make your own choices when you have internalized the relevant symbol
connections.

The Tarot Garden

FLOWERS

The Tarot draws upon a number of floral symbols. These include the rose. This is an ancient and universal symbol in its own right. The combination of beauty and pain through the flower and the thorn make the rose a natural symbol for life itself. The red rose represents manifestation. We find it on Trump I. We find the symbolism of the rose in many traditions. Roses were sacred to Isis in the Graeco-Roman phase of her worship. In the story *The Golden Ass* the hero Lucius is transformed from animal to human shape by eating from the garland of roses carried in the procession by the high priest. The Virgin Mary is called the rose of heaven. We find the five-petalled rose on the banner held by the figure of Death in Tarot Trump XIII.

The white lily by contrast symbolises purity. It was by tradition the flower of the annunciation. We see both roses and lilies upon the garments worn by the tonsured monks at the feet of the Hierophant.

The laurel is seen in the wreath of Trump XXI, the World and also in the cap of the Fool on Trump 0. This is easily identified as a symbol of victory. It is an evergreen, always a symbol of immortality. In Christianity the laurel represents the crown of martyrdom.

The iris flower refers to the lesser known Greek goddess Iris. Her name means rainbow. She is usually shown winged and bearing a herald's staff. Iris is the female counterpart of Mercury, the messenger of the gods. We find the iris on Trump XIV, Temperance.

We find four sunflowers on Tarot Trump XIX, the Sun. They reinforce the generally sunny and bright theme of this card.

The many-seeded pomegranates were sacred to Demeter, the earth mother. The pomegranate symbolizes fertility. We find pomegranates on Tarot Trump III, the Empress. We also see them on the veil behind the High Priestess on Tarot Trump II. This correspondence clearly refers to the fecundation within the spirit not within matter.

TREES

We find trees depicted throughout the Tarot. On Trump VI, the Lovers, we find two trees. Behind Eve we see the Tree of Life, the Tree of the Knowledge of Good and Evil with its fruit and serpent. Behind Adam we see another tree with twelve lights ablaze. It is reminiscent of the Biblical burning bush.

We find another tree on Trump XII, the Hanged Man. It is shaped in the form of a T. It represents the Tree of Sacrifice whether Christian or pagan. Christ was crucified. Odin hung on the World Tree Yggdrasil for nine nights.

On Trump III, the Empress, we see lush vegetation in the background. Here are cypress trees sacred to Venus.

WATER

The Tarot makes extensive use of water symbolism. We see it first in the icy peaks behind the Fool. It is suggested in the flowing blue folds of the robe worn by the High Priestess. We catch a glimpse of a great sea in the background behind a veil. A stream flows behind the Empress. The angel of Trump XIV, stands with one foot on the land, the other is dipped into a pool. In Trump XVIII, the Moon, a creature crawls from a pool onto the land. In Trump XVII a naked figure takes water from a pool and pours it onto the land. Coffins float upon a great sea in Trump XX. The Hermit treads the icy wastes in card IX. Death on a pale horse faces us in the fore-ground of Trump XIII. In the background a river flows.

Water symbolizes life. Pools of water represent the well springs of life. When flowing it represents the flow of life. Conversely it may also represent the boundary between states of life and death. The River Styx provided a symbolic boundary to the Greek mind. The great seas seen on Trumps II and XX represent not the source of life but the accumulation and culmi-nation of life. The great seas, like the collective unconscious, represent a collective experience and potentiality. Ice is water in a transformed state. The act of pouring water introduces a dynamic activity. The life energies are being circulated. Water nourishes the land and symbolizes the harmony within a balanced landscape. Water is widely used in traditional religions to symbolize purification, baptism and rebirth.

EXERCISE 14

What qualities, functions and powers do you ascribe to the element of Water?

Cosmic Symbols

THE MOON

We find that Tarot uses lunar symbolism both directly and indirectly. Tarot Trump XVIII is commonly called the Moon. Its esoteric title, Lord of the Waters of Flux and Reflux indicates the active relationship between the pull of the moon and the flow of the tides. The moon plays an important part in mythology and folklore. It is connected with pregnancy, the growth of plants and the reproduction of animals. The moon has traditionally been connected with women. The horned crown worn by the priestess in Trump II, the High Priestess, shows the phases of the moon which look like horns in the sky. Tarot Trump VII, the Charioteer, has moon epaulettes.

EXERCISE 15

What qualities, functions and powers do you ascribe to the moon?

THE STARS

The night sky has many mysteries. The stars have always fascinated. Like the moon, mythology and folklore tells the traditional stories of stars. There are many stories concerning the constellations of the zodiac. The stars represent an enigmatic power which takes us beyond the confines of our world. People have always wondered about the stars. Today scientists know a great deal about the lives of stars. Our own sun of course is a star. There are many other such stars in the heavens.

There is the canopy of stars in Trump VII. The Charioteer reminds us of the vastness of creation. The Charioteer is crowned with a star. The Empress seen on Trump III is also crowned with stars. The seven stars in the sky in Trump XVII refer to the seven lights, the chakras which hold the blueprint for personal unfoldment.

THE SUN

Our world receives its light and warmth from the sun. Our seasons and daily pattern result from our relationship to the sun. Solar symbolism is universal, The sun represents the source of life itself. We find solar images on Trump XIX, the Sun. Here a radiating sun beams life and warmth.

EXERCISE 16

What qualities function and powers do you ascribe to the sun?

Trump XIII, Death, shows us a rising sun appearing between two pillars clearly symbolizing the rebirth of life. We see the winged sun emblazoned on the chariot in Trump VII, Lord of the Triumph of Light. This too is a sign of rebirth.

We also find a white sun in Tarot Trump 0, The Spirit of Aethyr. This is a Qabalistic reference to the White Head, a name assigned to Kether, the source upon the Tree of Life.

Fabulous Beasts

We find a strange composite creature on Tarot Trump X, the Wheel of Fortune. The beast clearly has a human body but an animal's head. The Hermanubis simply represents the fact that humanity is still evolving. The lower aspects have taken on a unique human quality. However, the centres within the brain are still undeveloped and have not yet become fully human.

The sphinxes seen pulling the chariot on Trump VII, are truly mythical beasts, combining the head of a man, the body of a bull, the feet of a lion and the wings of an eagle. The four elements of Earth, Air, Fire, and Water are symbolized by the sphinx. The chariot is pulled by one black and one white beast symbolizing polarity and balance. We also see the Sphinx as Guardian of the Wheel of Becoming in Trump X. Oedipus had to face the riddles posed by the Sphinx.

The Tarot Zoo

The lion is called the king of the beasts. The lion symbolizes power, strength and has solar connections. We see a woman holding open the mouth of a lion on Trump VIII, Strength. Like Daniel in the lion's den she is quite unharmed. The innocence and purity of spiritual power have dominion over the vital life forces.

The symbolism of the serpent is ancient and universal. The extraordinary shedding habit of the snake is a powerful symbol of rebirth. We see the serpent behind Eve in Trump VI, Children of the Voice, Oracle of the Mighty Gods. It is curious to note that according to the system of Gematria which accords number values to individual letters, Nepesh the serpent and Messiah have an numerical equivalence.

In Trump I, we see that the Magus of Power wears a serpent belt. The serpent's tail is grasped in the mouth. This represents the injunction 'To be Silent'.

EXERCISE 17

What qualities, functions and powers do you ascribe to the serpent?

The Tarot also contains a number of minor but significant animal symbols. The ibis seen on Tarot Trump XVII is sacred to Thoth, the Egyptian Lord of Wisdom. The dog found on Tarot Trump 0, leaping beside the Fool is of course traditionally 'man's best friend' and a symbol of domestication. By contrast, the wolf seen on Tarot Trump XVIII symbolizes wildness. It is the ancestor to the dog, the root from which the domesticated dog family has sprung. In the same Trump, we see a crayfish. Here is a symbol of primitive and ancient life. The donkey in Tarot Trump XIX symbolizes humility. It has none of the grandeur or pedigree of the horse. We find the horse on Tarot Trump XIII. Here is a powerful mythological beast which appears in folklore and mythology throughout the world.

The Elements

EARTH, AIR, FIRE, WATER

The concept of the four elements is repeatedly expressed through the series of Trumps. In Trump I, the Magician we see the elemental weapons laid upon the table. The cup, sword, rod and pantacle symbolize the qualities, functions and powers of Earth, Air, Fire and Water. This quaternary itself represents a totality.

We find the four elements again on Trump X, the Wheel of Fortune. Here we see the four fixed signs of the zodiac Leo, Taurus, Scorpio and

Aquarius represented by the lion, the bull, the eagle and the man. The final Trump XXI, The World, again shows us the totality represented by the four elements. An understanding of the elemental foundation of the Tarot is essential if we are to penetrate beneath the surface.

We have already discovered various correspondences. It is now time to draw them together.

TABLE 6
CORRESPONDENCES

Element	Direction	Angel	Elemental Weapon	Tarot Suit
Earth	North	Uriel	The Pantacle	Suit of Discs
Air	East	Raphael	The Sword	Suit of Swords
Fire	South	Michael	The Rod	Suit of Wands
Water	West	Gabriel	The Cup	Suit of Cups

EXERCISE 18

Draw a circle. Place the names of each element in each quarter. What do you discover about the elements as a unity?

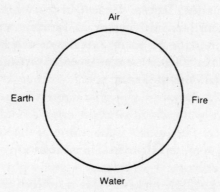

Fig. 7. The Circle of the Elements

Architecture

We find that the Tarot includes several strong architectural themes. Columns are shown on Trumps II, V and XI. The column does not belong to domestic architecture. It is clearly reminiscent of the temple, the church or other buildings of state.

The columns on either side of the High Priestess are deliberately depicted to suggest the two columns of the Temple of Solomon, Boaz and Jachin. The columns shown on Tarot Trump V, the Hierophant, are of the same colour. The decorated finials are deliberately designed to suggest the reproductive system, the physical source of life. The markings upon the columns represent souls moving both in and out of incarnation in a continuous flow. The columns on either side of the figure of Justice are suggestive of the powers of state. They are plain and simple without decoration or symbol.

We find stonework suggested repeatedly throughout the Tarot sequence. Columns and cubes, walls and thrones are hewn from stone. Here is the Qabalist's delight, to show one thing and to mean another. The word for stone in Hebrew is *ehben*. It is spelt *abn*. *Ab* refers to the Father, itself a name for the Divine Wisdom, and *Bn* refers to the Son, a name revealing yet another complex of associations and ideas. The simple image of 'stone' in fact refers to the Divine Union between the Divine Wisdom and the human race.

Yet another seemingly innocuous artefact is the stone cube which reappears on various Tarot Trumps. The Priestess is seated on a cube. The cube is a complex and important Qabalistic symbol. It derives from the enigmatic Qabalistic work, *Sepher Yetzirah*. In this work each of the letters is assigned a position in space. Together the arrangement forms a cube. A cube therefore symbolizes the totality of the meanings attributed to the Hebrew alphabet. The High Priestess is seated upon a cube of stone, a symbol of completed Divine Union.

Tarot Trump XV shows us a double cube. The archetypal man and woman are chained to the Devil who sits upon a double cube. Here is a very subtle reference. The double cube is one of the symbols assigned to Malkuth. Malkuth represents physical manifestation. The double cube rightly belongs to Malkuth. If we espouse a philosophy which chains us to matter, we make a devil for ourselves. It is clear from the imagery that the individuals could easily be freed by simply lifting off the chains. They are in fact imprisoned only by internal limitations. Matter has become the ruler and in doing so is transformed from the Being of Light within matter to a fiendish creation.

Symbols of Sovereignty

The figures of the Tarot frequently bear the symbols that we normally associate with royalty. Thrones and sceptres, shields and orbs, crowns and robes lift the focus of our attention away from the mundane world. The attributes of royalty refer us not to monarchies and earthly rulers but to archetypal forces and powers. Both the Empress and the Emperor carry insignia of office. The Emperor bears an orb and sceptre, the Empress carries a sceptred orb. They are both crowned and throned within their own kingdoms. The Hierophant by contrast bears a staff indicating spiritual authority.

The Magus of Power and the Lord of the Triumph of Light bear remarkably similar staffs. These short-tipped, wand-like lightning conductors transmit power from one plane to another. Finally the figure of the World bears two such rods, one in each hand. Spiritual power and material form are balanced and eternally present.

Landscapes

The sequence of Tarot Trumps taken together represents a journey. It is not surprising that we should therefore find the recurring image of a path.

The path itself is a universal symbol of the spiritual life. Buddhism speaks of the Lam Rim, the graduated path towards enlightenment. Yoga speaks of the Marga, the Path or Way. In the Western Mysteries the Path is to be found in the twenty-two byways and the Sephiroth of the Tree of Life,

In Tarot Trump 0, the Fool is clearly about to take the first step. We do not see the path. The path lies ahead somewhere in the future. Nevertheless, here is the starting point of the journey represented by the Tarot,

In Tarot Trump VI, we see both the path and the mountain. The meandering lowlands represent the early stages of the spiritual path. Here the terrain is gentle and pleasant. Perhaps the traveller does not realize that the looming mountain will have to be climbed too. We see a mountain in the background of Trump VIII, Strength.

We see the same image in Tarot Trump XIV, Temperance. These images, however, are distinctly Qabalistic and refer to a specific path and its internal experiences. On Tarot Trump XVIII, the Moon, we also see a pathway which emerges from a pool and finally disappears into a mountain range in the distance. This is the path of biological evolution.

EXERCISE 19

What meaning can you discover in the concept of 'The Path'?

Frozen peaks and icy wastes appear on several Tarot Trumps. We meet them first in the background behind the Fool. At the outset of the journey this frozen condition represents potentiality. The Hermit too treads a whitened and barren landscape. He has travelled far and experienced all the conditions that life can offer. The totality of his experiences places him beyond the delusions offered by the world. He travels alone. Lastly we see icy wastes in the background of Tarot Trump XX, Judgement. Here the frozen condition represents the grip of delusion which freezes life and encases the individual in an icy stupor.

The process of integrating even a single symbol cannot be hurried. Firstly, it has to be intellectually analysed and recognized in different forms. Secondly, it has to be intuitively explored through free association. Thirdly, it has to be internalized and integrated as a living part of the psyche.

Symbols unlike words offer an unlimited series of associations and connections. Complex human realities such as love, suffering, death are merely limited by words. A symbol points to the impossibility of defining these vast experiences through simple descriptions. We need to understand symbols both intellectually and intuitively. We need to understand how symbols have served culture and religion. We must also come to our own understanding of symbolic language.

CHAPTER THREE

Archetypes and Meanings

The Tarot then is a symbolic wheel of human life.
Paul Foster Case

The student new to Tarot frequently tries to memorize long lists of meanings. The attempt is doomed to failure. This approach uses memory at the expense of understanding. There is no need to memorize lists of meanings. There is a need, however, to understand the archetypes. Each Tarot Trump represents a basic life experience or theme. This may be loosely defined as the archetype, 'Contents and modes of behaviour that are more or less the same everywhere and in all individuals. It is, in other words, identical in all men and thus constitutes a common psychic substrate of a suprapersonal nature which is present in every one of us.'[1] In other words each Tarot Trump depicts an aspect of the human experience that is common to all. An individual life is quite unique, yet we are each born, we will each die, we are created by the action of male and female, we each live our unique journey finding both successes and failures and ultimately we come to know ourselves. These basic patterns are common to all human life. They are imprinted deep within collective understanding.

The Archetypal Patterns

The contents of the collective unconscious, on the other hand, are known as archetypes.
Carl G. Jung

These archetypal patterns can be identified at both transpersonal and personal levels. At the collective level the archetype is not personalized. For instance, the universal experience of birth is common yet transpersonal. However, the individual experience of birth will be intensely personal. We can see how the transpersonal and the personal levels are connected yet distinct.

An archetype manifests in the following sequence.

1. **The Primal Archetype:** collective, unconscious, transpersonal, for example, the Feminine.
2. **The Secondary Archetype:** collective, conscious, transpersonal, represented through its sacred symbol, for example, the symbolic representations of the Feminine as goddess.
3. **The Personal Complex:** personal, unconscious, individualized, experienced through feelings and powerful emotions, for example the emotional and affective response to womanhood.
4. **The Personal Meaning:** personal, conscious, individualized, experienced through feelings, emotions, integrated into everyday life, for example, the private comprehension of womanhood.

These four levels connect the transpersonal archetype to daily life and personal experience. Let us take an example. Death is a universal experience. This primal archetype has been rendered into an infinite number of symbolic forms. We are familiar with 'the grim reaper' and 'the ferryman'. Every society has its own cultural symbols which serve as a shorthand for this experience. At the personal level, when we are touched by the event, we experience it through our feelings and emotions. These emotions may be so powerful that we are unable to think clearly. With understanding we are able to integrate the experience into the fabric of our lives. We come to an understanding of its meaning. There is unbroken line of connection between the archetype and the everyday experience of it.

If we apply this same fourfold analysis to each Tarot Trump, we need to ask two questions. Firstly, we need to ask, 'which archetype is being presented?' Secondly, we need to ask, 'How does this archetype appear in everyday life?' If we apply these questions to each of the Tarot Trumps, we will come to understand both the archetype and the mundane meanings. We do not have to resort to memorized lists. However, this does not mean that we have no interior work to do. We have to begin by recognizing and exploring the archetype.

The Sacred Seven

Everything in the unconscious seeks outward manifestation, and the personality too desires to evolve out of its unconscious condition and to experience itself as a whole.
Carl G. Jung

After a week's meditation on retreat Strephon Kaplan Williams formulated a model to show the interrelationships between archetypes. This model is extremely valuable as a means for exploring the Tarot Trumps. The symbols which traditionally represent seven archetypes are to be found representing the Tarot Trumps.

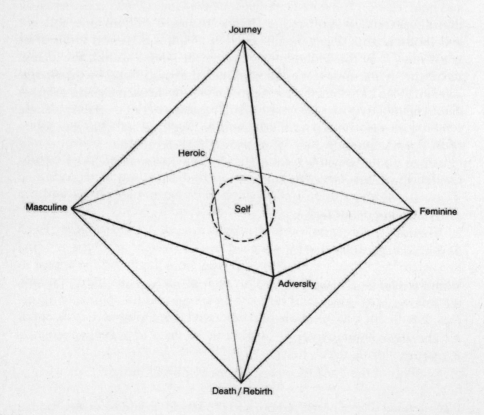

Fig. 8. The Seven Archetypes

The First Archetype – The Self

Transforming into new being by separating and integrating the opposites which underlie existence.
Strephon Kaplan Williams

The search for Self lies at the heart of all true spiritual journeys. A classic meditation repeatedly poses this question and concludes with the answer, 'I am not my body, I am not my emotions, I am not my thoughts. I am a centre of pure consciousness.' If we are content to identify fully with the body, the emotions or the mind, we accept an incomplete and unbalanced self model. The Self transcends these partial definitions. The Self is one. It is the transformative centre of the psyche.

The individuation process, the drive to become one's true self originates here. This drive is the Magnum Opus, the Great Work. 'It constitutes a magnificent endeavour, but certainly a long and arduous one and not everybody is ready for it.'[2] Symbolically, the Self is expressed in terms of wholeness. It is the Philosopher's Stone, the divine union, the divine child, the divine androgyne. The Self may be symbolized by a butterfly, an animal, the kingdom, the mystic rose, the ring, the sacred circle or mandala. The Self may also be symbolized as a diamond or a rainbow. These symbols are not the dry stuff of scholarly language, but the vocabulary of an inner language which speaks through the dream life.

When we examine the symbolism of Tarot Trump 0, the Fool, we can identify the following symbols:

1. The androgynous figure.
2. The rose.
3. Sacred circles depicted on robe.

When we look at Tarot Trump XXI, the World, we are able to identify the following symbols:

1. The androgynous figure.
2. A ring.
3. Symbols of the Four Elements, representation of unity.

It is intended that of both the Fool and the World should be understood as figures representing androgyny. The Fool represents the beginning of the journey, the World represents the completion of the journey. These

Trumps also contain further linking imagery. The Fool wears a green cap with a red feather as he/she steps over the abyss. The figure of the World is set within an oval laurel wreath bound with red as he/she steps and dances.

The Tarot opens and closes with the symbolism of the Self. The Fool is taking the first step of the journey. The World dances at the centre. The journey is complete. The Self is one. The Self and the World have become one through a mysterious journey of transformation. We cannot become identified with the Self, the centre of pure consciousness unless we are willing to undertake the journey.

EXERCISE 20
1. Lay Tarot Trumps 0 and XXI side by side. Meditate on the symbolic connections that you can discover between the two Trumps.
2. How would you symbolize the Self?

The Second Archetype – The Feminine

Dwelling within by being perpetually open to all aspects of life and death.
Strephon Kaplan Williams

The Feminine is a powerful archetype. We are all born of the mother. The Feminine is universally represented in all sacred traditions; literature, iconography and myth. Her faces are many and varied. She is a goddess bestowing gifts, a hideous witch offering a warning, a temptress testing a young man's fidelity. The Feminine always functions as initiator into the emotional nature. She can be harsh to the unawakened who refuse her tests. Commonly in a fairytale scenario, three sons set out on a journey. An old woman challenges them with a seemingly impossible task. The two elder sons invariably fail. They are shown to be too self-centred, inflexible and unwilling. The youngest son accepts the challenge with a good heart and eventually is successful. The Feminine demands an openness to experience, a willingness to face initiation.

The symbolic representation of the archetype is familiar; the Wise Woman who offers cryptic instruction to the questing knight, the seductive witch/siren who attempts to turn the hero from the quest, the goddess who bestows her favours. These are all faces of the Feminine. Symbolically we can recognize the Feminine presence through vessel and cave, cauldron and cup, throne and veil, moon and water, as queen and princess, goddess and wisdom-woman, as bestower of love, fertility and secrets.

When we look at Tarot Trump II, the High Priestess, we can identify the following symbols:

1. A crowned, enthroned, feminine figure.
2. A veil decked with pomegranates, symbols of fertility.
3. Lunar symbols.
4. Water.
5. The scroll, symbolic of Wisdom Teachings.
6. Dominance of the colour blue, referring to water symbolism.

When we look at Tarot Trump III, the Empress, we can again identify undeniable symbols:

1. A crowned, enthroned, feminine figure.
2. Symbols of sovereignty, crown and sceptre.
3. Symbols of fertility, corn.
4. Symbol of love, the shield of Venus.
5. Robe decked with pomegranates.
6. Running water.

When we look at Tarot Trump XVII, the Star, we again find a female figure. We are able to identify the following symbols:

1. A naked female figure.
2. Water as a pool and as a stream being poured onto the land,
3. Stars.
4. Open landscape.
5. Bird and tree.

When we look at Tarot Trump VIII, Strength, we can identify the following symbols:

1. A female figure.
2. The sign of infinity.
3. A lion.
4. A distant mountain.

When we look at Tarot Trump XI, Justice, we find a depiction of the Greek Titaness Themis. We find the following symbols:

1. A crowned and enthroned female figure.
2. A veil.
3. Columns.
4. Sword and scales.

EXERCISE 21
   1. Lay out Tarot Trumps II, III, VIII, XI, XVII. Meditate on any connections you can discover between them.
   2. How would you symbolize the Feminine?

The Third Archetype – The Masculine

Knowing the goal and doing what is necessary to achieve it.
C.G. Jung

The polar opposite of the Feminine is clearly defined as the Masculine. The gender war which still rages, generally dislikes both stereotype and archetype, confusing one with the other. These patterns are best comprehended as neutral powers of equal value. The concept of Yin and Yang expresses a relationship between fundamental polarities. These terms are not intended as limitations of individual behaviour any more than terms such as stasis and entropy. They are intended to describe forces in action, one for expansion, the other for containment.

Culturally, the Masculine most often appears as the hero, a guise which evokes a common emotional response. The Masculine usually appears in tales of kingship contest as both the king and the wise old man or wizard. Mythologically the kingdom provides a background for the interplay of the whole range of archetypes. The ills of patriarchy are often laid at the door of the unbridled Masculine. Traditional symbols of the Masculine presence include the sword, the king, the wise man, the phallus, the sun, the sceptre, a standing stone, saviour gods.

When we look at Tarot Trump IV, the Emperor we can identify the following symbols:

1. A crowned and throned king.
2. Symbols of sovereignty.
3. The symbolism of the ram.
4. Solar colours – red, yellow, and orange.

When we look at Tarot Trump I, the Magician, we can identify the following symbols:

1. A standing male figure.
2. The symbol of infinity.
3. The phallic wand.
4. The table of the elements.
5. The serpent girdle.
6. Roses and lilies.

When we look at Tarot Trump V, the Hierophant, the Magus of the Eternal, we can identify the following symbols:

1. A seated and enthroned male figure.
2. Symbols of sovereignty.
3. Ritual vestments.
4. Roses and lilies.
5. Keys.

When we look at Tarot Trump XIX, the Sun, we can identify the following symbols:

1. The Sun and rays of sunshine.
2. Four sunflowers.
3. A child with a feather riding a horse.
4. A stone wall.

When we look at Tarot Trump IX, the Hermit, we can identify the following symbols:

1. The rod.
2. The wise old man.
3. The light.
4. The journey.

EXERCISE 22
1. Lay out Tarot Trumps I, IV, V, IX, XIX. Meditate on the symbolic connections that you can discover between them.
2. How would you symbolize the Masculine?

The Fourth Archetype – The Heroic

Achieving mastery by bringing resolution to the chaotic and the split.
Strephon Kaplan Williams

The heroic myth is universal. Here is an archetype to which we all respond. Story, whether in film or theatrical form, still draws upon the heroic ideal with great success. Indiana Jones is a contemporary hero in a world easily divided into good and evil, black and white. Classical myths feature the adventures of the hero in the same way. Heracles, Jason and Odysseus are classical forefathers to our own heroic idols from stage, screen and the real world. The hero brings hope. The victory brings a new order, balance is restored. The hero faces the adversary and is triumphant. As a cultural symbol, the hero can become identified with national aims and aspirations, a dangerous departure from the true heroic ideal which is truly selfless and without guile. The hero's sacrifice is a genuine expression of compassion.

Traditional heroic symbols include: the just warrior, youth, triumphal marches, garland and spoils, the great heart, the battle, the healing, the sacrifice, the ordeal.

When we look at Tarot Trump VII, the Chariot, we can identify the following symbols:

1. The chariot and charioteer.
2. The sphinxes.
3. A winged sun.
4. Stars.
5. A walled city.
6. A phallic wand.

When we look at Tarot Trump XII, the Hanged Man, we find the heroic theme expressed through redemptive sacrifice.

We find the following symbols:

1. A man suspended by one foot.
2. A tree.
3. A shining halo.

EXERCISE 23
1. Lay out Tarot Trumps VII and XII. Meditate on any connections you can discover between them.
2. How would you symbolize the Hero?

The Fifth Archetype – Adversity

That which limits and destroys all things.
Strephon Kaplan Williams

As any child knows, a story includes 'the goodies' and 'the baddies'. As any adult knows, life is never straightforward. Everyday experience includes challenges, obstacles, frustrations, crises and problems. These difficulties present themselves, they are not chosen. These unwanted circumstances appear to offend our sense of good order, being both chaotic and random. It is no surprise then that adversity appears in the guise of the adversary, the enemy. We can only respond by rising to the occasion, summoning all our strength and courage. In effect we have to take on the persona of the Hero ready to do battle with the adversary. It is not difficult to see how adversity has become personalized into the adversary.

Christianity has expelled its image of the adversary. The Tempter represents all that is evil and wicked. Tibetan Buddhism on the other hand is rich with demonic forms which are fully integrated into the whole. These images enable the individual to understand, encounter and personally integrate aspects of the adversary. Traditional symbols for adversity are the monster, the devil, the demon, darkness, imprisonment, plague and sickness.

When we look at Tarot Trump XV, the Devil, we identify the following symbols:

1. A devil.
2. Chains.
3. Darkness.
4. Male and female prisoners.

EXERCISE 24
1. Lay out Tarot Trump XV, the Devil. What do you discover about it?
2. How would you symbolize Adversity?

The Sixth Archetype – Death/Rebirth

Crisis and revolution, the transition in which one thing becomes another.
Strephon Kaplan Williams

We yearly watch the cycle of death and rebirth through nature. Yet we remain gripped by fear at our own mortality. Death and rebirth have become separated. Death/rebirth is in reality a continuous daily event. Body cells die and are replaced. As our ideas change, we are in effect reborn into new levels of consciousness. Initiation represents a quantum leap in consciousness. Initiation is often represented through symbols of death and rebirth. The initiate is often called 'the twice born'. Death and rebirth are intimately and inextricably bound. They form an inseparable unity.

Traditional symbols for this process are the rising sun, transformation, the phoenix, new plant life, images of initiation, symbols of death and resurrection together.

When we look at Tarot Trump XIII, Death, we can identify the following symbols:

1. Death.
2. The land of the living.
3. The land beyond life.
4. The rising sun.
5. The five petalled rose.

When we look at Tarot Trump XVI, the Tower, we can identify the following symbols:

1. A tower.
2. Male and female figures.
3. Darkness.
4. A bolt of lightning and a crown.
5. Images of destruction.

EXERCISE 25

1. Lay out Tarot Trumps XIII, XVI. Meditate on any connections you can discover between them.
2. How would you symbolize Death/Rebirth?

The Seventh Archetype –
The Journey

The way and steadily evolving direction forwards.
Strephon Kaplan Williams

The spiritual search is often described as a path. As was said before, Buddhism describes the graduated path towards enlightenment as the Lam Rim. Yoga describes its tradition as Marga, the Way. Alice Bailey, amanuensis to the Tibetan, writes: 'The path is, therefore a path on which steady expansion of consciousness is undergone with increasing sensitivity to the higher vibrations.'[3] In the West we find that the Tree of Life offers a route divided into thirty-two paths. The symbol of the spiritual path is a perfectly natural one. It implies conscious choice, a beginning, a destination and the journey itself. The path has many different phases each with its own difficulties and tests. Sometimes the path is broad and meanders through the plains. At other times the ascent is steep and daunting.

It is therefore no surprise to find images of journeying in the Tarot. Traditional symbols include: mountains, the Tree of Life, pathways, rivers, oceans, guides/divine presences, pilgrimages, the wheel, images of the quest and images of the cycles of life.

When we look at Tarot Trump VI, the Lovers, we can identify the following symbols:

1. The path.
2. The mountain.
3. Trees.
4. A guiding presence.
5. Male and female figures.
6. Two towers.

When we look at Tarot Trump XIV, Temperance we see the following symbols:

1. A path.
2. Two mountains.
3. The rising sun.
4. A guiding presence.
5. A pool.

When we look at Tarot Trump XVIII, the Moon, we can identify the following symbols:

1. A pool.
2. A path.
3. A mountain range.
4. Animals.
5. The personified moon.

When we look at Tarot Trump X, the Wheel of Fortune, we can identify the following symbols:

1. A wheel.
2. Symbols of the four elements representing unity.
3. A serpent.
4. An armed sphinx.
5. A composite creature being carried by the wheel.

When we look at Tarot Trump XX, Judgement, we find the following symbols:

1. A great sea.
2. A guiding presence.
3. Men, women and children.

EXERCISE 26

1. Lay out Tarot Trumps VI, X, XVIII, XX. Meditate on any connect-ion that you can discover between them.
2. How would you symbolize the Path?

The Primal Archetype

When we examine the fruits of our analysis, we can attribute the Tarot Trumps to a primal archetype.

TABLE 7
ARCHETYPES AND TAROT TRUMPS

The Self	The Fool, The World
The Feminine	The Moon, Strength, The Empress, The High Priestess, The Star, Justice
The Masculine	The Magician, The Sun, The Hermit, The Emperor, The Hierophant.
The Heroic	The Chariot, The Hanged Man
Adversity	The Devil
Death-Rebirth	The Tower, Death
The Journey	The Wheel of Fortune, The Lovers, Temperance, Judgement

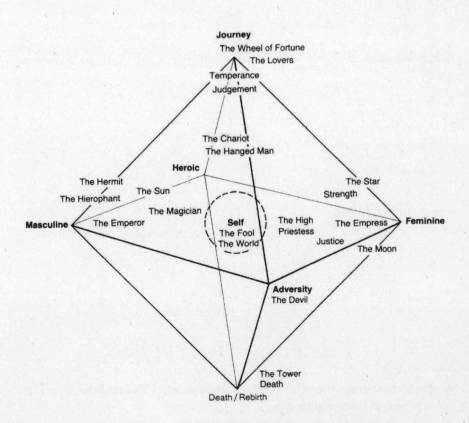

Fig. 9. The Tarot Trumps and Archetypes

We have identified the archetypes presented through the Tarot. When we recognized the archetype, we can interpret its symbolic representation and understand how it will operate in ordinary life. Our original schema, like a ladder, connects the primal archetype to everyday life. We can look at each Trump in the light of this fourfold analysis.

Let us begin by asking the following questions:

1. What archetype is being presented?
2. How do I recognize it?
3. How does the archetype affect life?
4. How will I feel when this archetype affects my daily life?

Let us now apply this analysis to Tarot Trump XVI as an example.

1. **Primal Archetype**
   Q. What archetype is being presented?
   A. Death–Rebirth.
2. **Symbolic Representation**
   Q. How do I recognize it?
   A. As Tarot Trump XVI, the Tower.
3. **Manifestation**
   Q. How does the archetype affect life?
   A. Destruction, fear, loss, eviction, failure, renewal, rebirth, new beginnings.
4. **Presentation**
   Q. How will I feel when this archetype affects my daily life?
   A. 'Everything I have worked for is crashing down around me.
      I am losing everything.
      My whole world is collapsing.
      I will rebuild my life.
      I will start again.
      I will recover
      Like a phoenix I will arise from the ashes.'

EXERCISE 27

Apply this schema to the Tarot Trumps in turn. For example:
1. **Primal Archetype**
   Q. What archetype is being presented?
   A. Adversity.

2. **Symbolic Representation**
   Q. How do I recognize it?
   A. As Tarot Trump XV, the Devil.
3. **Manifestation**
   Q. How does the archetype affect life?
   A. Imprisonment, captivity, loss of autonomy, misery, trials.
4. **Presentation**
   Q. How will I feel when this archetype affects my daily life?
   A. 'I feel helpless.
      I feel powerless.
      The adversary appears formidable.
      Circumstances are against me.
      How will I find the strength to fight this situation?
      What must I do to win my freedom?'

When you are analysing the Trumps in this way, you will find that you naturally and readily respond to certain Trumps while others simply leave you cold.

EXERCISE 28
   1. List all the Trumps to which you spontaneously relate.
   2. List all the Trumps to which you feel immediate resistance.

You may find that these same resonances are mirrored in your natal chart.

Meanings

It may come as a surprise to learn that the primary reason for divination in the Great Work is not to learn the future. Rather it is for the development of psychic faculties.
Robert Wang

There is no need to attempt to commit long lists of meanings to memory. Instead if you have completed the interior work, the meanings will naturally be apparent to you. The connection between the common divinatory meanings and archetypal essence should be clear to you from the following list:

Trump 0: The Fool   Archetype – The Self
   Divinatory Significance – A beginning, originality, spirituality, folly
   and eccentricity in material matters
Trump I: The Magician   Archetype – The Masculine
   Divinatory Significance – Constructive power, initiative, skill, activity,
   cleverness
Trump II: The High Priestess   Archetype – The Feminine
   Divinatory Significance – Wisdom, fluctuation, secrecy, things hidden,
   deep issues, intuition
Trump III: The Empress   Archetype – The Feminine
   Divinatory Significance – Fertility, fruitfulness, abundance, happiness,
   maternity
Trump IV: The Emperor   Archetype – The Masculine
   Divinatory Significance – Stability, power, reason, control, authority,
   ambition
Trump V: The Hierophant   Archetype – The Masculine
   Divinatory Significance – Revelation, the influence of organized religion,
   spiritual teachings
Trump VI: The Lovers   Archetype – The Journey
   Divinatory Significance – Love, partnership, personal relationships,
   marriage, inspiration
Trump VII: The Chariot   Archetype – The Heroic
   Divinatory Significance – Triumph, victory, success, self-assertion,
   travel
Trump VIII: Strength   Archetype – The Feminine
   Divinatory Significance – Courage, spiritual strength, self-mastery,
   fortitude
Trump IX: The Hermit   Archetype – The Masculine
   Divinatory Significance – Wisdom, the lone pioneer, prudence, inner
   counsel, divine inspiration
Trump X: The Wheel   Archetype – The Journey
   Divinatory Significance – The cycles of life, an unexpected turn, a
   change
Trump XI: Justice   Archetype – The Feminine
   Divinatory Significance – Legal affairs, justice, a judgement, decision
Trump XII: The Hanged Man   Archetype – The Heroic
   Divinatory Significance – Surrender, an act of sacrifice, unconven-
   tional behaviour
Trump XIII: Death   Archetype – Death/Rebirth
   Divinatory Significance – The end of a phase, a new beginning,
   transformation

Trump XIV: Temperance   Archetype – The Journey
  Divinatory Significance – Balance, partnership, good prospects
Trump XV: The Devil   Archetype – Adversity
  Divinatory Significance – Bondage, material desires, a trial, obsessions
Trump XVI: The Tower   Archetype – Death/Rebirth
  Divinatory Significance – Failure, the crash of expectations, re-
  evaluation, unfulfilled ambition
Trump XVII: The Star   Archetype – The Feminine
  Divinatory Significance – A blessing, hope, insight, a gift, a promise
Trump XVIII: The Moon   Archetype – The Feminine
  Divinatory Significance – Organic change, hidden currents, uncer-
  tainty, dissatisfaction
Trump XIX: The Sun   Archetype – The Masculine
  Divinatory Significance – Enlightenment, joy, success, prosperity
Trump XX: Judgement   Archetype – The Journey
  Divinatory Significance – Decision, change of direction, final settle-
  ment, waking up
Trump XXI: The World   Archetype – The Self
  Divinatory Significance – Completion of a cycle, success, achievement,
  the matter of the question

EXERCISE 29
  Create your own divinatory meanings for each Trump.

CHAPTER FOUR

Letters and Numbers

*Thus the letters of the Hebrew alphabet, because they are nouns are
actually twenty-two labels for mental pictures.*
Paul Foster Case

Unlike our own language which has no symbolic quality, each Hebrew
letter is part of a complete symbol system. Each letter is itself a symbol.
Even the shape of the letter frequently reinforces the implicit symbolism.
Furthermore each letter also has a numerical value. In the same way that a
child delights in concealing secret messages by converting words into
numbers, the Qabalist seeds a treasure trail of abstract spiritual messages in
number code. If a code breaker takes the time and applies the effort necessary to decode the cypher, then worth is proven and the treasure is won.
The treasure is protected in its number guise from the profane and the
ignorant.

The twenty-two Hebrew letters were originally assigned to the twenty-
two Paths upon the Tree of Life. The attribution of the Tarot Trumps to
the Paths is a relatively recent attribution. In many ways the more accessible Tarot images have overshadowed the earlier significance given to the
letters. When Tarot Trumps were combined with Hebrew letters, two
independent symbol systems of extraordinary complexity meshed
together. It is not surprising that the relationship between Tarot images
and Hebrew letters is still on occasion a matter of considered debate
among Qabalah aficionados.

We need to grasp the basic symbols before moving on to their application or we shall find ourselves being swamped by symbols, correspondences and attributions.

TABLE 8
THE HEBREW LETTERS

Name	Letter	Numerical Value	Symbol
Aleph	א	1	an ox or bull
Beth	ב	2	a house
Gimel	ג	3	a camel
Daleth	ד	4	a doorway
Heh	ה	5	a window
Vau	ו	6	a nail
Zain	ז	7	a sword
Cheth	ח	8	a fence or enclosure
Teth	ט	9	a serpent
Yod	י	10	the creative hand
Kaph	כ	20	the palm of the hand
Lamed	ל	30	an ox goad
Mem	מ	40	water
Nun	נ	50	a fish
Samekh	ס	60	a prop, support
Ain	ע	70	an eye
Peh	פ	80	a mouth
Tzaddi	צ	90	a fish hook
Qoph	ק	100	the back of the head
Resh	ר	200	the front of the head or face
Shin	ש	300	a tooth
Tau	ת	400	a cross

The Sepher Yetzirah

Although The Sepher Yetzirah is the fundamental text book of the Qabalah, most, if not all the Cabalists are baffled by this work, finding it mysterious, occult and well-nigh incomprehensible.
Carlo Suares

The Book of Creation is surrounded by paradoxes.
Irving Friedman

The *Sepher Yetzirah* is a brief book, no more than a booklet in fact. It is composed of no more than 250 lines, divided into six chapters. *The Book of Formation* or *Book of Creation* must rank among the most cryptic works ever written. 'Throughout the centuries, it has had an influence out of all proportion to its size, leaving an indelible mark on Western thought.'[1]

Eliphas Levi described the *Sepher Yetzirah* as 'a ladder formed of truths.'[2] It is here that we first encounter the term *sephiroth*.

In the work, the twenty-two Hebrew letters represent the process of creation. In Chapter 11, this basic theme is established. 'Twenty-two foundation letters: He ordained them, He hewed them, He combined them, He weighed them, He interchanged them. And he created with them the whole creation and everything to be created in the future.'[3] The twenty-two letters are divided into three groups; the three Mother Letters, the seven Double Letters and the twelve Simple Letters. Each type of letter is perceived to be quite different in function.

The Autiot – The Mother Letters

The foundation of all others is composed of the Three Mothers, Aleph, Mem and Shin.
Sepher Yetzirah, Chapter 3

The autiot therefore arrange themselves in equations not words.
Carlos Suares

The Hebrew word for the letters is *Autiot,* in the singular, *Aut.* This name denotes a letter but also a sign, proof, symbol and even miracle. Clearly if a single letter may denote a miracle, we are deep in realms metaphysical.

These three letters have a special significance. Each letter represents an elemental creative power.

> He caused the letter Aleph to reign in the Air and crowned it, and combining it with the others He sealed it, as Air in the World as the temperate (climate) of the Year, and as the chest in man. He caused the letter Mem to reign in Water, crowned it, and combining it, with the others formed the earth in the world, cold in the year and the belly in man, male and female. He caused Shin to reign in Fire, and crowned it, and combining it with the others, sealed with it the heavens in the universe, heat in the year and the head in man, male and female.[4]

In the Tarot sequence the Mother Letters are assigned to Tarot Trumps 0, XII and XX. Aleph, elemental Air is assigned to the Fool, The Spirit of Aethyr. Mem, elemental Water is assigned to the Hanged Man, Spirit of the Mighty Waters. Shin, elemental Fire is assigned to Judgement, The Spirit of Primal Fire. We can already see a correspondence between the symbolism of the Mother Letters and the esoteric nature of the Trumps. We can only come to appreciate any significance between the letters and the Tarot Trumps through personal meditation and reflection.

EXERCISE 30

1. Take each of the Mother Letters and the appropriate Tarot Trump. What connections can you discover between each letter and its Trump?

For example, Aleph, elemental Air, cosmic prana, the Fool, Spirit of Aethyr, transcendent pre-matter, the particles of the subatomic level perhaps.

The Seven Double Letters

He preferred the number seven above all things under heaven.
Sepher Yetzirah, Chapter 1

There are seven Double Letters in the Hebrew alphabet. They are Beth, Gimel, Daleth, Kaph, Peh, Resh and Tau. According to Chapter 4 of the *Sepher Yetzirah*,

> These Seven Double Letters He designed, produced and combined, and formed with them the Planets (stars of this Universe) the Days of the Week, and the Gates of the Soul in Man. From these Seven He hath produced the Seven Heavens, the Seven Earths, the Seven Sabbaths; for this cause He has loved and blessed the number Seven, more than all things under Heaven.

The Double Letters are also assigned to directions. These letters are each attributed both twin sounds, a soft and hard pronunciation, and twin qualities.

This extraordinary amalgam permits the complex to be conveyed on the back of the simple. Combinations of letters can express ideas, abstract concepts and philosophical ideas. 'Each letter reproduces a number, an idea and a form; so that mathematics are capable of application to ideas and to forms not less rigorously than to numbers, by exact proportion and perfect correspondence.'[5]

TABLE 9
ATTRIBUTION OF THE DOUBLE LETTERS

Letter	Polarity	Direction	Body Part	Planet
Beth	Life/Death	Above	Eye	Sun
Gimel	Peace/War	Below	Eye	Venus
Daleth	Wisdom/Folly	East	Ear	Mercury
Kaph	Riches/Poverty	West	Ear	Moon
Peh	Grace/Indignation	North	Mouth	Saturn
Resh	Fertility/Solitude	South	Nostrils	Jupiter
Tau	Power/Servitude	Palace of Holiness	Nostrils	Mars

The seven Double Letters and the qualities attributed to these letters are assigned to the Tarot Trumps in the following way:

TABLE 10
ATTRIBUTION OF DOUBLE LETTERS, TRUMPS, QUALITIES

Letter	Trump	Name	Quality
Beth	Tarot Trump I	The Magician	Life/Death
Gimel	Tarot Trump II	The High Priestess	Peace/War
Daleth	Tarot Trump III	The Empress	Wisdom/Folly
Kaph	Tarot Trump X	The Wheel of Fortune	Riches/Poverty
Peh	Tarot Trump XVI	The Tower	Grace/Indignation
Resh	Tarot Trump XIX	The Sun	Fertility/Solitude
Tau	Tarot Trump XXI	The World	Power/Servitude

If our understanding of the Tarot Trumps is to be enriched by this correspondence, we need to discover the relationships between the individual Trumps and the qualities represented by the polarity. Certain relationships show themselves at once. Representing a window, Heh is clearly connected to the function of sight. Lamed represents an ox goad. It is obviously related to the function of work. These correspondences can deepen our understanding of the Trumps to which they are assigned.

EXERCISE 31

Take the polar qualities assigned to each of the Double Letters. What can you discover in the relationship between the Trumps and these attributions?

For example, Power and Servitude represent ways in which we may react to the world. When I meditate on the use of Power I must also meditate on Servitude, is this service or servility? If Tau symbolizes the Palace of Holiness within the self, then I may choose to project either Power or Servitude. Which one shall I choose?

The Twelve Simple Letters

He made them for strife; He arrayed them as for battle.
God set one against another.
Sepher Yetzirah, Chapter 5

The twelve simple letters of the alphabet are Heh, Vau, Zain, Cheth, Teth, Yod, Lamed, Nun, Samekh, Am, Tzaddi and Qoph. A month of the year, a sign of the zodiac, an internal organ, a direction and a function is assigned

TABLE 11
ATTRIBUTION OF THE TWELVE SIMPLE LETTERS

Letter	Symbol	Function	Direction	Zodiac	Organ
Heh	Window	Sight	North-East	Aries	The Right Hand
Vau	Nail	Hearing	South-East	Taurus	The Left Hand
Zain	Sword	Smell	East Above	Gemini	The Right Foot
Cheth	Enclosure	Speech	East Below	Cancer	The Left Foot
Teth	Serpent	Taste	North Above	Leo	The Right Kidney
Yod	Hand	Sexual Love	North Below	Virgo	The Left Kidney
Lamed	Ox goad	Work	South-West	Libra	The Liver
Nun	Fish	Movement	North-West	Scorpio	The Spleen
Samekh	Tent peg	Anger	West Above	Sagittarius	The Gall Bladder
Am	Eye	Mirth	West Below	Capricorn	Large Intestine
Tzaddi	Fish Hook	Imagination	South Above	Aquarius	Stomach
Qoph	Back of the Head	Sleep	South Below	Pisces	Small Intestine

to each of these letters to create an extraordinary interweaving of corre-spondences, both human and cosmic. It is impossible to absorb the meaning of these relationships except through meditation. We have already seen how each letter is assigned to a direction. When projected in the mind this curious correspondence creates a three-dimensional figure in the form of a cube. The Cube of Space is a model for contemplating relationships. Its form can be created through concentrated visualization. This is not a simple exercise and is best offered to those with considerable mental control and substantial experience. However, even the less experi-enced meditator can use the structure as a framework for thought by simplifying the number of correspondences to be included.

The Cube of Space

The Cube of Space is a kind of three-dimensional Mandala that can help us, in our three-dimensionally conditioned consciousness, to formulate, contact and cope with further dimensions.
Gareth Knight

Anyone who can follow a subway map of New York City will have no problem with the Cube of Space.
Robert Wang

In Chapter 1 of the *Sepher Yetzirah*, we find that God sealed the universe in six directions giving height, depth and the east, west, north and south. The letters of the alphabet are assigned to each act of creation. The seven

Fig. 10. The Cube of Space

Double Letters are established in seven cardinal localities including the central point marked out by the letter Tau. The twelve Simple Letters are allotted to the directions which form the boundaries between the six faces. These directions 'diverge to infinity, and are as the arms of the universe'.[6] This model of creation is envisaged as a cube with its six faces and central point. If you have the commitment, this model can be built into the psyche over a period of time. Like any inner model, what you get from it will be directly proportional to what you put into it.

Creating the Cube of Space

Before we begin the work of building in the creative imagination we need first to orientate ourselves to the implicit presence of the three Mother Letters, Aleph, Mem and Shin. These are not specifically a part of the structure. Nevertheless they represent the background which supports the structure and should not be ignored.

Gareth Knight suggests that we 'see ourselves building our Cube of Space "within" the letter Aleph, looking beyond it to Shin for our authority and inspiration, and expecting the results of our actions to be reflected ultimately in the substance of Mem'.[7]

These are wise and indeed practical words of advice. Neglecting spiritual principles is to court spiritual pride. Use the three Mother Letters as a means of establishing your intent before you commence the work of creating the Cube of Space.

EXERCISE 32

Imagine yourself standing in space. The letter Tau shines at your heart. Direct your attention upwards to see the first face of a cube forming above you. In the centre shines the letter Beth, meaning a house. Look down towards your feet. See the second face of the cube forming beneath you. The letter Gimel shines in its centre. Here is the ship of the desert, the camel to bear you on your travels both inner and outer. Directly ahead of you in the East, the third plane forms, inscribed with the glowing sign for a doorway, Daleth. Here is the doorway of the Dawn, the light of spiritual illumination. Now turning your attention to the north at your left, see the fourth face of the cube forming. It is inscribed with the letter Peh, meaning a mouth. Here is a sign of communication and speech. Behind you in the West, the fifth plane forms. Its letter is Kaph, the open receiving palm of the hand. Finally on your right in the South, the final plane forms. The letter Resh shines brightly. It symbolizes the front of the head, representing the development of self consciousness.

The structure of the cube is now in place. Meditate within it until you are familiar with its faces, directions and letters. Imagine that each of the faces begins to move away from you, moving out to the farthest reaches of the universe. You remain in the centre at the Palace of Holiness. The Tau still shines at your heart.

If you wish to add the Simple Letters proceed only when you have integrated the experience of the Double Letters which form the boundaries between the six faces. Using the guide as an aide memoir, establish the four letters Teth, the Serpent of Wisdom, Samekh, the support, Zain, the Sword and Tzaddi, the fish hook. Each image should be used as a focal point for meditation. Turning to the face below, inscribed with Gimel, establish the four letters, Cheth the enclosure, Yod, the hand, Qoph, the back of the head and Am the eye. Turning to the northern face, establish Teth, the

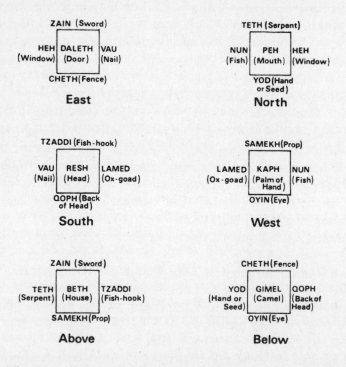

Fig. 11. The Faces of the Cube. Directions and Letters (from Experience of the Inner Worlds by Gareth Knight)

serpent, Nun the fish, Heh the window and Yod, the hand. Turning to the West establish Samekh, Lamed, the ox goad, Nun and Am. Turning to the South establish Tzaddi, Vau, the nail, Lamed and Qoph.

The Cube of Space is a complex exercise. It should not be hurried or it will simply fail to have any personal value. The work should proceed slowly and with due reflection and meditation at every stage. This exercise has the power to initiate the individual into the Hebrew letters and the Tarot Trumps to which they are attributed. Though the exercise is lengthy and will test your powers of application as well as your visualization skills, the technical construction of the form is secondary to the inner spiritual reconstruction which proceeds with the work.

Above all we must remember the central point of the Cube of Space we have built, which is sometimes referred to as the Holiest Point. It is in fact the human heart. And the fact of doing things from the heart, instead of through intellectual curiosity or social convention, or whatever, adds another whole dimension to our magical operation.[8]

Secret Codes

The Hebrew alphabet is so rich in symbolic associations that the simple act of spelling a word can establish an enigma, a code. Using the language in this way has always been a Rabbinical delight. We see this most clearly in the Tetragrammaton, of course. But it also applies to other words. By applying what we already know of the relevant symbols, we can discover how meaning is encoded with form.

The letters of the Tetragrammaton are separately assigned to Trumps.

1. The letter Yod is assigned to Tarot Trump IX, The Hermit.
2. The letter Vau is assigned to Tarot Trump V, The Hierophant.
3. The letter Heh is assigned to Tarot Trump IV, The Emperor. This letter is used twice in the formula.

The Yod signifies the creative hand, its shape is likened to the sperm. Yod is called the 'paternal' letter. It is unashamedly masculine by nature. It is assigned to the Sephirah Chokmah, the Primal Father. When we apply these images to the figure of the Hermit travelling alone in the icy waters, we can realize that here is an image of archetypal Wisdom. The name Chokmah is translated as Wisdom. Here is a further confirmation that the Hermit is indeed the Wise Old Man. The grey cloak of the Hermit reinforces his connection with the Sephirah Chokmah. Its colour in a commonly used scale is grey. Here we touch on the intricacies and subtleties of Qabalistic riddling. Paul Foster Case, founder of the group, the Builders of the Adytum, composed a book of verse meditations on the Hebrew letters. These have much to offer the committed student of Tarot and Qabalah. A selection of verses from the *Book of Tokens* relating to the four letters of the Tetragrammaton might prove insightful to the student.

Yod

Therefore do the wise see in the letter Yod
The fatherhood of Chokmah
The unbounded Wisdom which establishes all.

Heh

Again, a window is set in the wall of a house,
Even as the eye is set in the head
They who dwell within may look abroad
To see what passeth without
Hence it is written in the Book of Formation
That the letter Heh correspondeth unto the faculty of Sight.

Vau

In all the universe there is no break.
By bonds indissoluble
Each point is fastened to every other.

Heh

Of mine own substance are all things made,
And I give myself freely to every one.
They know me truly who see
That it is my nature to bring forth
And to originate.

… This whole universe
Is an expression of my primal will to yield fruit.

EXERCISE 33

Take each verse as a theme for meditation.

As the relationships between the letters and the Trumps are often subtle, we need to deepen our understanding both intellectually and at an intuitive level. Grasping the symbolic relationships presented through these associations requires some personal work and thought. If the relationships were merely logical deductions, there would be no need to encode them within a symbolic language. There is much to be discovered here given intellectual application and intuitive realization.

TABLE 12
LETTERS AND TRUMPS

Letter	Tarot Trump
Aleph	Tarot Trump 0, The Fool
Beth	Tarot Trump I, The Magician
Gimel	Tarot Trump II, The High Priestess
Daleth	Tarot Trump III, The Empress
Heh	Tarot Trump IV, The Emperor
Vau	Tarot Trump V, The Hierophant
Zain	Tarot Trump VI, The Lovers
Cheth	Tarot Trump VII, The Chariot
Teth	Tarot Trump VIII, Strength
Yod	Tarot Trump IX, The Hermit
Kaph	Tarot Trump X, The Wheel
Lamed	Tarot Trump XI, Justice
Mem	Tarot Trump XII, The Hanged Man
Nun	Tarot Trump XIII, Death
Samekh	Tarot Trump XIV, Temperance
Ain	Tarot Trump XV, The Devil
Peh	Tarot Trump XVI, The Tower
Tzaddi	Tarot Trump XVII, The Star
Qoph	Tarot Trump XVIII, The Moon
Resh	Tarot Trump XIX, The Sun
Shin	Tarot Trump XX, Judgement
Tau	Tarot Trump XXI, The World

EXERCISE 34

What connections can you discover between each of the Hebrew letters and the Trumps to which they are assigned? For example, the letter, Tzaddi and Trump XVII, the Star Tzaddi represents a fish hook and the power of the Imagination. I see a pool which I take to be the universal mind. If I wish to fish in these waters, I must develop the patience of the Fisherman. I must make my mind like a fish hook, ever ready for the catch. The mental powers of the Imagin- ation (much undervalued by modern society) seem here to be much valued. When I have applied my mind then perhaps the goddess Nut will bless me.

Numbers

It is the purpose of all cyphers to invest a few signs with much meaning.
Carlo Suares

Numbers have always been the Qabalist's delight, a truly secret cypher. The twenty-two letters of the alphabet have a numerical value. This relationship permits the straightforward translation of words into numbers. However, the deeply symbolic nature of the Hebrew letters in fact enables one symbol system to be rendered into another. The practical possibilities of encoding complex metaphysical notions into a code of numbers was a Rabbinical joy which resulted in the creation of three systematized approaches.

Firstly Gematria evolved from the relationship between numbers and letters. Words of the same number were deemed to have a necessary connection. Secondly the system of *Notaricon* which took its name from Latin *notarius*, meaning a shorthand writer, became an extraordinary esoteric shorthand. A single word was constructed from the initial, or even final, letters of the several words of a sentence. A sentence might also be constructed using words each beginning with the letters of a given word. Finally the system of *Temura*, meaning permutation, involved the letters of a word transposed according to certain rules. Such extraordinary and abstruse pastimes are of little concern to anyone except those who chose to follow such specialities. However, the existence of such obscure yet systematized approaches clearly reveals the Qabalistic mind at work.

Some familiarity with the basic esoteric principles behind numbers will, however, serve the student of Tarot. If we are to comprehend the esoteric significance attached to numbers, we must see numbers as geometric realities. In other words, we need to see a number in relation to the geometry which is inseparable from it. The numbers 0–10 can best be understood with reference to the Tree of Life. Each Sephirah is assigned a number which expresses its essential nature.

I am One which transforms into Two
I am Two which transforms into Four
I am Four which transforms into Eight
After all of this, I am One.
Words of Thoth

THE NUMBERS OF THE TREE OF LIFE

0	**The Ain Soph**	The Limitless Light. An ellipse representing the cosmic egg. Zero is the symbol of absence of qualities. It is a sign of infinite and eternal conscious energy. In it are included all possibilities but it transcends them all. It is the Void itself without form, yet the source of all form.
1	**Kether**	The first point of manifestation. The point of beginning. Unity.
2	**Chokmah**	The line created by two points. Polarity. Duality.
3	**Binah**	The triangle created by three points. The first stable figure. Development. Growth.
4	**Chesed**	The square created by four points. Measurement.
5	**Geburah**	The pentagram. The possibility of motion. Adaptation. Versatility. Five is dominant in the substructure of living forms.
6	**Tiphareth**	The cube. The hexagon. Balance. Equilibrium. Beauty. Harmony.
7	**Netzach**	An especially important creative number, six circles of the same size, arranged in a circle will leave space for a seventh circle of the same size in their midst.
8	**Hod**	The octave. Rhythm. Alternate cycles. Eight is characteristically found in the geometry of mineral or inanimate structures.
9	**Yesod**	Transition.
10	**Malkuth**	Manifestation. Completion, fulfilment.

This schema provides our means of understanding the meanings attributed to the Minor Arcana. The Four Suits are placed on the Tree of Life in corresponding numerical order so that the Aces, the Roots of the Elemental Powers, are placed in Kether, the Twos in Chokmah, etc. The Tens are of course placed in Malkuth. This allocation provides our key to understanding the pip cards. Each card draws its meaning from the interaction between the nature of the Sephirah and the nature of its own suit.

We do not have to attempt to memorize long lists of meanings for the Minor Arcana cards. If we understand the key principle we can derive the meaning for ourselves. We need first to remind ourselves of the essential characteristics of the elements as represented by the four suits. Fire is a highly spiritual power. Air is elusive yet omnipresent. Water is fluid and ever moving. Earth is solid and tangible. From this brief and oversimplified analysis we can anticipate how these powers will interact at various levels of the Tree of Life. Elemental Fire representing Spirit will resonate easily at the higher levels but will become increasingly less at ease as the descent into matter deepens. The Ten of Wands is Oppression. Elemental Earth on the other hand sits easily in Malkuth manifestation. The Ten of Discs is Wealth. The Element of Water is also ill at ease within the form represented by Malkuth. There is a conflict between the stability of earth and the movement of water. The Ten of Cups is Satiety, saturation. The Ten of Swords is Ruin, the power of the intellect taken to its logical, extreme and absurd conclusion in this the most concrete of the Sephiroth.

We may see the same principles at work in the Sephirah of Tiphareth at the centre of the Tree. Tiphareth serves as a transforming and uniting force in this central position. Its energies represent a position of balance and equilibrium. Accordingly we find that each of the sixes shares something of this harmony. The Six of Wands is Victory; spirit has not yet descended into form. The Six of Swords is Science; the mind is applied to discovery and to rational knowledge. The Six of Cups is Pleasure; harmony prevails. The Six of Discs is called Success; equilibrium is stabilized at this central point on the Tree.

One further example will serve to add to our understanding of both Tree and Tarot. By contrast with Tiphareth, the fifth Sephirah Geburah is abrasive and catabolic. According to the principles that we have established we can expect the Fives to represent disruption. The Five of Cups is Disappointment. The Five of Wands is Strife. The Five of Swords is Defeat. The Five of Discs is Worry. Once again we cannot fully understand the inner workings of Tarot unless we appreciate its relationship to the Tree of Life.

If we are to understand the Qabalistic view of numbers we have to move on from the idea of numbers as mere enumerators and instead look to universal laws expressed through mathematical relationships such as the Golden Mean and the Fibonacci series where we will find fascinating corroboration of Qabalistic notions.

TABLE 13
THE TREE AND THE MINOR ARCANA

Sephirah	Discs	Swords	Wands	Cups
Kether	Ace of Discs	Ace of Swords	Ace of Wands	Ace of Cups
Chokmah	Change	Peace	Dominion	Love
Binah	Work	Sorrow	Virtue	Abundance
Chesed	Power	Truce	Completion	Luxury
Geburah	Worry	Defeat	Strife	Disappointment
Tiphareth	Success	Science	Victory	Pleasure
Hod	Failure	Futility	Valour	Debauch
Netzach	Prudence	Interference	Swiftness	Indolence
Yesod	Gain	Cruelty	Strength	Happiness
Malkuth	Wealth	Ruin	Oppression	Satiety

The Pattern of the Trestleboard was devised as an aid to remember the main attribution of the numbers 0–10. It is offered here in the same spirit.

These eleven affirmations 'have proved their value as seed-ideas, which planted in the mind by thoughtful and purposeful repetition, bear rich fruit in mental and spiritual unfoldment'.[9]

THE PATTERN OF THE TRESTLEBOARD

0   All the power that ever was or will be is here now.

1   I am a centre of expression for the Primal Will-to-Good which eternally creates and sustains the universe.

2   Through me its unfailing Wisdom takes form in thought and word.

3   Filled with Understanding of its perfect law, I am guided moment by moment along the path of liberation.

4   From the exhaustless riches of its Limitless Substance, I draw all things needful both spiritual and material.

5   I recognize the manifestation of undeviating Justice in the circumstances of my life.

6   In all things, great and small, I see the Beauty of the divine expression.

7   Living from that Will, supported by its unfailing Wisdom and Understanding, mine is the Victorious Life.

8   I look forward with confidence to the perfect realization of the Eternal Splendour of the Limitless Light.

9   In thought and deed, I rest my life, from day to day, upon the sure Foundation of Eternal Being.

10   The Kingdom of the Spirit is embodied in my flesh.

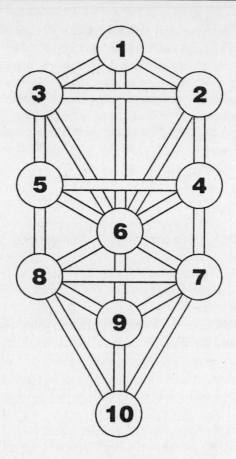

Fig. 12 The Tree of Life With Numbers

Sacred Signs

*Each letter of the Hebrew alphabet represents a specific number. Each
one signifies an aspect of living forces at play in the Universe and the
text is intended to project these forces into our very being, thus acting
as a Revelation.*
Carlo Suares

The Mysteries of the Hebrew alphabet still exert a powerful fascination.
Currently Stan Tenen, Director of Research for the Meru Foundation
presents an exciting and original thesis which combines sacred letters,
mathematical forms and cosmology.[10] He suggests that the letters themselves

originated in the gestures and shapes made with the human hand. The individual letter therefore conveys its unique meaning through gesture. Furthermore, these gestures express the same principles of creation described through another language by mathematicians and physicists.

Carlo Suares too has indicated the cosmic nature of the principles embedded in these letters. As we have already seen, the letters of the alphabet are assigned number values in the following way.

Aleph to Teth	1–9
Yod to Tzaddi	10–90
Qoph to Tau	100–400

According to Suares, 'the first nine letters are archetypes of numbers from 1–9'.[11]

| 1 | Aleph | Archetype of life-death abstract principle of all that is and all that is not. |
| 2 | Beth | Archetype of all containers, the physical support without which nothing is. |

Fig. 13. The Hebrew Letters Derived from Shadowgrams
(© Stan Tenen/Meru Foundation)

3	Gimel	Archetype of the organic movement of every Beth animated by Aleph.
4	Daleth	Archetype of physical existence as response to life.
5	Heh	Archetype of universal life.
6	Vau	Archetype expressing the fertilizing agent.
7	Zain	Archetype of the achievement of every vital impregnation.
8	Cheth	Archetype of unstructured substance, the storage of undifferentiated energy, the most unevolved state of energy.
9	Teth	Archetype of primeval female energy which builds into structures.

Suares describes Beth as the archetypal container. In a similar fashion Tenen ascribes *the mark of distinction*, a mathematical concept, to Beth. Mathematically this distinguishes *inside* from *outside* and provides the first logical distinction, an absolute necessity for the unfolding of archetypal symmetry.

The letters/numbers from Yod to Tzaddi describe 'the process of the nine archetypes in their factual conditioned existence: their projections in manifestation are always in multiples of 10. The nine multiples of 100 express the exalted archetypes in their cosmic states.[12] The number 1000 is written with an enlarged Aleph. It is seldom used, representing tremendous cosmic power. The twenty-two letters are supplemented by the following letters described by the term 'final'.

The Final Letters

Kaph	ך	500
Mem	ם	600
Nun	ן	700
Peh	ף	800
Tzaddi	ץ	900

Here we have a complete code, signs which can be read as both numbers and words. The historical usage of this is fascinating but highly complex. We can do little more than point towards certain highlights. An example from a work by Paul Foster Case, *The True and Invisible Rosicrucian Order* may reveal the intricate and subtle thread of meaning which leads through a maze of interconnected letter, number and geometric symbols.

'They say that *Malkuth* is the Resplendent Intelligence, and the adjective *resplendent* is written MThNVTzO in Hebrew. The numbers of these letters add to 656; hence the word shows numerically the characteristic figure of initiation. Represented geometrically, 656 shows the pentagram, symbol of Man, between two hexagrams, symbols of the forces of the universe, thus: ✿☆✿ Therefore, 656 represents the idea that man is the mediator and adapter, set between the infinite and the eternal cosmic Past and the infinite and eternal cosmic Future. Moreover, 656, is the number of the Hebrew noun ThNVR, *thanoor* (furnace), which is the derivation of the alchemical term *athanor*, defined as "a self feeding, digesting furnace, wherein the fire burns at an even heat". This *athanor* is the human body. Its fire is the fire of life, and this is the fire that the Zelator, or alchemist's assistant, must learn to control and regulate.[13]

The following might be of interest to the student.

1. The Tetragrammaton YHVH; Y = 10, H = 5, V = 6, H = 5, total = 26
2. A cube has 6 sides, 8 corners and 12 edges, total = 26
3. The four fixed signs of the zodiac, as houses 2, 5, 8, 11, total = 26
4. The four Sephiroth of the Middle Pillar, 10+9+6+1, total = 26
5. The number of the square 4, plus the number of the circle 22, total = 26
6. The noun *Maftayakh* meaning Key is rendered MPTHCH, total = 528 which is the sum of all the numbers from 1 to 32.

EXERCISE 35

Using the number code transliterate the following words into their numerical equivalents:
1. Ruach Elohim (RVCH ALHIM) The Life Breath of the Gods or Spirit of God.
2. Nachas (NChSh) serpent, snake.
3. Mashiach (MshYCh) messiah.

The student may investigate as deeply as interest and time permit. It is an area of infinite possibilities and profound insights.

CHAPTER FIVE

Doorways and Keys

To have the benefit of this wonderful invention, the Keys must be inside you. This means that you must be able to call up the images of any Key by a simple act of will. When you can do this, the Tarot will be part of your very flesh and blood, and it will begin to effect far reaching transformations in your thinking and thus in your living.
Paul Foster Case

When the keys to the Tarot have been integrated every Trump becomes a doorway. When every Trump becomes a doorway, Tarot becomes a vehicle of initiation. In the true spirit of the Western Mysteries, this process is self-driven. It is a process of self-revelation. We receive from the teacher within. Neither Tarot nor Qabalah offer dogma or offer any pre-set answers. The symbolic language poses both puzzle and solution. It is the student who determines both the nature of the puzzle and its resolution.

Tarot images capture the imagination in exactly the same way as a powerful dream or even a sophisticated brain teaser. We have a need to make sense of the dream. We want to solve the puzzle. However, resolving the dream may be important but its meaning is likely to be highly personal. The brain teaser may be intellectually, even intuitively, satisfying but its resolution will not change your life. Resolving Tarot symbols into a meaningful pattern *will* change your life. It will bring you into personal contact with the archetypal themes of human existence. It will initiate you into the collective mind.

The application of the intellect alone will bring a partial and unsatisfying understanding. The application of the intuition alone will bring only a haphazard and fragmented appreciation of the archetypal symbols. However, the intellect and the intuition together lead us towards initiation. We need to prepare ourselves for this future experience by orientating our work in this direction from the outset. We need to cover the work of both Stage 1 and Stage 2 in anticipation that Stage 3 will spontaneously take place through an appropriate vehicle.

Stage 1 Analysis – Intellectual Study
Purpose: To Understand the Inner Construction of the Tarot Trumps
Undertake:
Analysis of each symbol.
Analysis of each Trump by symbol.
Analysis of each Trump in relation to the Tree of Life.
Analysis of mythological characters where appropriate through background reading.

Stage 2 Synthesis – Intuitive Expansion
Purpose: To Understand the Inner Meaning of the Tarot Trumps
Undertake:
Synthesis between individual symbols.
Synthesis between symbols relating to each Trump.
Synthesis between individual Trumps.

Stage 3 Osmosis – Active Absorption
Purpose: To Confer the Tarot Initiation
Undertake:
Programme of meditative integration using the universal models
The Cube of Space
The Tarot Trumps
The Tree of Life
Dynamic enactment, that is, *The Journey of the Fool*.

Awakening The Intuition – Meditation

Meditation within the aid of the Tarot is a helpful and valuable practice because it is founded on the experimental realities and laws of the human psyche. It is an active practice involving all components of the personality physical, mental and intuitive without shutting any out.
Stephen Hoeller

Intellectual study is familiar territory; education actively promotes these skills. Awakening the intuition is unfamiliar territory; education actively discourages such skills. Dynamic enactment, active meditation, is foreign territory; education has lost these skills. Meditation is the key discipline for awakening the intuitive mind. It cannot be avoided. Meditation serves to prepare the mind for intuitive leaps, initiation. Without meditation initiation cannot and will not take place. We therefore have to begin with the practice of meditation if we are seriously committed to Tarot studies. We have to think in a new way. This process is no different from any other new learned experience. We have to face a learning curve. We have to create a new mental framework.

Meditation is an ancient mental discipline. It is a mistake to think of it purely as an Eastern system. Meditation is universal. Meditation is most simply understood by comparing the practice to a target. It is our intention to hit the target, that is to keep the mind focused upon the subject of the meditation, the target. The further our thoughts stray from the subject, the further we have wandered from the target. The theory is simple; the practice is a little more difficult. The attention wanders, the concentration fails, the mind strays far and wide from the target. However, with practice distractions lessen, concentration increases and the intuition opens. Initially it feels as if a great deal of intellectual effort is required to distil a single intuitive droplet. In time this balance shifts so that a small intellectual trigger releases a flood of intuitive realizations. However the process cannot be rushed. There are no short cuts on this inner journey.

Every meditation will produce a result. Sometimes the result is imperceptible, no more than an improvement in concentration or a lessening in distractions. However, once concentration has become fairly reliable, the result of the meditation becomes more tangible, a realization takes place in the mind. Quite simply, 'the penny drops'. It is important to keep a record of all meditations and their realizations. A realization can take many forms, it may come as an inner voice, a symbols a new comprehension. It may come as the meditation proceeds, it may appear some hours later. The realization may even appear in a dream some weeks later. The realizations are often fleeting and barely conscious, much like dream images upon waking.

If you are committed to your own initiation, it is essential that you establish firm foundations from the outset. You should meditate regularly, recording your realizations in a Tarot Diary. Diary keeping is highly personal. Nevertheless this diary should follow a structure which will permit steady inner growth. Your meditations will form the foundation for your own initiation. If you have not taken the trouble to make these foundations secure your own initiation will be delayed or, even worse, unstable. Each symbol presented by the Tarot is like a brick. When each brick has been laid securely in place, it is possible to construct a wall. It is not possible to construct a building without connecting bricks in an appropriate order. It is not possible to pass through an initiatory experience until the inner symbolic connections have been made. You will need to work through Stage 1, Analysis and Stage 2, Synthesis. Like a snowball gathering speed, the cumulative results of both intellectual and intuitive expansion precipitate Stage 3.

Doorways

Think of a door, a very old wooden door with massive iron hinges, try to see it as clearly as you can in your mind's eye. Take your time and look at every detail, the pattern of the wood, the darker burls where there has been a knot hole, the marks of the plane and the chisel.
Dolores Ashcroft-Nowicki

Meditative work on the Trumps should proceed on an orderly and regular basis. The following approach can be adopted after the student has acquired an intellectual framework. This approach requires the active use of the imagination. This should not be confused with pretence and invention. By holding an image clearly in the mind, we internalize the focus of our attention. Creating the image is not, however, the purpose of the exercise, it is the vehicle through which an intuitive realization may occur. The realization spontaneously arises through the experience of dwelling upon the image. It appears as something over and above the input, in this case the Tarot Trump. The mind is engaged in a dual task; creating the image and watching the inner reaction to the image.

OPENING THE DOOR

1. Select the Trump you wish to work with. Have the relevant Trump in front of you.
2. Enter a meditative state. Visualize the Tarot Trump clearly in your mind.
3. Allow the image to grow so that the frame of the Trump becomes a doorway.
4. Step into the image. Deepen your meditative state. What can you learn from this Tarot Trump? When the meditation is finished, step back through the image, reduce it to a proper size and return all images to a passive state.

5. Record your experience straightaway.
6. Do not attempt to encounter more than one image during a single session.

The following diary entries show realizations at the three levels, intellectual understanding, intuitive realization and initiatory experience.

Stage 1

Meditation subject: Tarot Trump 0, The Fool, The Spirit of Aethyr

Looked at the clothing worn by the Fool, counted ten circles – the Sephiroth, so he is a carrying the Tree as he journeys. Noticed two other symbols on his robe, one seems to be a flame, this reminds me of the symbol for Spirit, the other one is the Hebrew letter Shin, which also represents Fire, need to think about the relationship between Fire and Spirit some more. Noticed that the Fool wears both white and black, this reminds me of opposites. I wonder why the background is yellow, will have to check this.

The Fool is wearing odd coloured tights, sort of yellow/green. Maybe this is citrine. Where have I read about that colour before, must check it out. Wondered what the Fool carries over his shoulder, what would I need for a long journey, a map perhaps. Is there a clue in the symbol of the eagle on the wallet? Eagles fly high and are renowned for good eyesight, is this a play on words eyesight/insight? The eagle is the higher sign for Scorpio, must read up on what Scorpio represents. I see a dog, must think about what this represents.

Stage 2

Meditation subject: Tarot Trump 0, The Fool, The Spirit of Aethyr

The Fool is journeying between the levels, setting out on a journey. He is about to descend into manifestation, to cross the Abyss. He bears the map upon his outer robe. The ten Sephiroth represent the totality of past, present and future. He carries it all. It will be unfolded as he journeys. The Fool is neither male nor female but Spirit, hence the title, the Spirit of Aethyr. He/she bears the triple flame and the Shin, Elemental Fire.

Stage 3

Meditation subject: Tarot Trump 0, The Fool, The Spirit of Aethyr

Entered through the doorway of the Trump. Saw the Fool on the mountain top. The air was brilliant and clear, with the feeling of being the first day in a new world. Saw a brilliant white sun in the sky, white like a magnesium flare too white to look upon. Felt like Moses before the burning bush afraid to look up yet overawed by a living presence. The Fool handed me the rose for a moment and spoke.

'All is to be unfolded as the white rose.' Then I returned it, thanking him for letting me hold it. I felt that he/she was joyful to be journeying and eager to be on his/her way. He/she radiated an extraordinary quality of innocence I have never experienced in another person. I was momentarily reminded of the innocence attributed to Christ.

'What have you to teach me?' I asked.

'That I am present in all things,' replied the Fool.

With that the Fool stepped forward and disappeared over the edge of the precipice. He seemed to leap in delight. Instantly the sky below was filled with colour and sound. It seemed that everything erupted like a gigantic fireworks display. I felt I had observed a new world coming into being. The Fool was gone, the journey had begun. I closed the meditation.

EXERCISE 36
Explore each of the Tarot Trumps in turn using this technique.

The Active Imagination

The imagination, is one of the most important and spontaneously active
functions of the human psyche, both in its conscious and in its
subconscious aspects or levels.
Robert Assagioli

It is only too easy to misunderstand the use of the word 'imagination'. It is too easy to associate it with the play of children and the world of make-believe. It is too easy to dissociate the imagination from the grown-up world of adults who have no time for pretence or child's play. This is a great loss. For the creative imagination truly puts us in touch with our own creative powers and indeed with the powers required to recreate ourselves. Jung's own encounters with the unconscious led him to pioneer the use of the active imagination as a valuable psychiatric tool. His own inner life led him to see the unconscious at work in dream material and in spontaneous fantasy. He later realized that the unconscious could also be seen at work in the artificially generated fantasy: 'fantasies produced by deliberate concentration'.[1] Jung's autobiography reveals his personal struggle with the powerful images and emotions which he discovered within himself. In order to both clarify and deepen his understanding Jung began to combine the active controlled imagination with his own spontaneously emerging visions. He wrote 'I frequently imagined a steep descent. I even made several attempts to get to the very bottom'.[2] It was during one of these attempts that he encountered two figures who called themselves Salome and Elijah. They dwelt together with a large black snake. At the time Jung could not understand their significance for him. Many years later and with hindsight he came to realize that Elijah represented the Sage, the Wise Old Man. Salome represented an erotic power. Later another figure called Philemon appeared. Philemon first appeared to Jung in a dream 'as an old man with the horns of a bull. He held a bunch of four keys, one of which he clutched as if he were about to open a lock. He had the wings of a kingfisher with its characteristic colours.'[3]

Speaking of Philemon, Jung wrote, 'in my fantasies I held conversations with him and he said things which I had not consciously thought'.[4] On reflection Jung realized that Philemon represented superior insight.

The active imagination was also suggested as an important personal tool by another pioneering psychologist, Robert Assagioli. He originated Psychosynthesis, a systemized approach to personal growth. According to Assagioli the imagination needs to be controlled when excessive and trained when weak. It needs to be regulated, developed and utilized.

Jung was also interested in particular techniques for strengthening the active imagination. He recognized that it functioned differently for different types of people. This same point has been taken up by a relatively new movement, Neuro-Linguistic Programming, NLP for short. Predominantly visual people see inner pictures with ease. Audio-visual types see pictures but also hear words and sentences which are perhaps disjointed at first. Predominantly auditory people hear dialogue but see pictures less clearly. Kinaesthetic people being highly tactile respond to sensation even using the imaginary function.

The ability to carry on an inner dialogue may at first seem extraordinary, even bizarre. Jung's familiarity with the unconscious enabled him to dialogue with unusual intensity and power. Yet Jung saw this ability as a mere development of a perfectly normal and everyday quality. 'There are, indeed, not a few people who are aware that they possess a sort of inner critic or judge who immediately comments on everything they say or do.'[5] Too often this behaviour is linked only with mental illness. 'Normal people too, if their inner life is fairly well developed, are able to reproduce this inaudible voice without difficulty, though as it is notoriously irritating and refractory it is always repressed. Such persons have little difficulty in procuring unconscious material and thus laying the foundation for the transcendent function.'[6]

Jung's experiences exactly mirror the Conclusions reached by Assagioli. He offered the use of the active imagination as a means of integrating the various levels of the self. Assagioli promotes the same techniques for transpersonal growth where we may encounter superior insight and aged wisdom. Assagioli suggests that the active imagination be channelled into a dialogue with a source of inner wisdom. The establishment of an inner dialogue is exactly what Jung spontaneously encountered. It is exactly what we offer through the Tarot Initiation.

The Inner Guide

He was a mysterious figure to me. At times he seemed quite real, as he were a living personality. I went walking up and down the garden with him, and to me he was what the Indians call a guru.
Carl G. Jung

Jung did not make an original discovery when he encountered inner figures. It is something that all travellers in higher consciousness come to discover for themselves. The Inner Teacher is universally recognized in all traditions by many different names. These personal encounters are, however, so charged, so numinous that those so touched by such an experience are profoundly changed and empowered.

Edwin C. Steinbrecher wrote *The Inner Guide* detailing his own encounters with various inner teachers. In 1969 Steinbrecher was himself in analytical psychology. He had been introduced to the technique of the active imagination and like all intrepid explorers he set out on his own. 'I attempted to do this by inventing a staircase in my imagination that would take me within to those archetypal images I was seeking.'[7] He duly reached the bottom of the staircase and met the High Priestess. Steinbrecher had made his first inner contact. He was charged by the potential that he encountered and developed a system of cross references between Tarot and astrology which utilized the inner guide as a means of altering personal dynamics. According to Steinbrecher,

> The Inner Guide Meditation is the product of the mingling of spiritual and philosophical streams: astrology, tarot, alchemy, analytical psychology, Qabalah and the Western Mystery Tradition which contains the Judaeo-Graeco-Christian spiritual heritage of the West. From this synthesis of potent currents comes a gestalt in which the Guides — humanity's lost teachers appear, fresh, alive and waiting to serve the individual quest; to lead us towards the 'Kingdom of Heaven' to be found within each of us.[8]

Steinbrecher's visualization for making the initial Guide contact includes the familiar journeying motif, not unlike Jung's own imaginary descent.

> Close your eyes, and invent a cave around you as if you had just walked into the cave and the entrance is at your back. Allow the cave to structure itself as it will, well-lighted or dim, smooth-walled or rough. Try to be like a blank film receiving impressions. Accept these impressions uncritically as they come to you from this environment. Try not to edit what comes.
>
> Be as *sensory* as you can. Is the cave moist or dry? Feel the weight of your body as you stand on the cave floor. What kind of floor are you standing on? Feel it with your feet. Is it flat and smooth or rough and uneven. Feel the texture of the floor under your feet. Is it sandy, rocky or gravelly? Feel the air around you. Are there currents, or is the air still? Smell the air. Notice the colour impressions that come to you. Use all your senses.
>
> ... When you can feel yourself in the cave, even though things may still be vague at this point, *move forward and to the left*, away from the cave entrance, and find some kind of doorway or opening there on the left that will take you out into a landscape.
>
> ... Again, take whatever comes uncritically, and move through the aperture presented by the unconscious. Take a step out into the landscape when it appears, feeling the new type of ground under your feet. Is it soft or hard, grassy or rocky? What is around you? What is the scene like? Let all these impressions come to you, and let them solidify.

... Then with your mind call for an animal to come to you. Let it be an animal you don't know ... and ask the animal to lead you *off to the right* to where your Inner Guide awaits.

... The animal will lead you to ... an unknown male figure – your first Guide. The initial Inner Guide for both men and women is a male form. (This is probably because the horoscopic area which describes his physical being and personality, the Ninth House, is associated with three masculine or *yang* energies) ... You will generally feel an outpouring of love, protection and friendliness from the figure.

Having met your guide: 'Ask the Guide to point to where the *Sun* is in the sky of your inner world. Look to where he points. Is the *Sun* right over-head or off to one side? Are there clouds, or does it shine in a clear sky?' Having located the Sun, 'Ask the *Sun* to come to you in human form'.[9] As the Sun exerts a primacy, it is encountered first. The Inner Guide may later introduce other archetypal powers to you.

Steinbrecher suggests presenting each archetype with the following questions:

1. What do you need from me and from my life to work with me and be my friend?
2. What do you have to give me that I need from you?

This inner dialogue accords with Jung's use of the creative imagination. The second question extends symbolism within the dialogue. It usually elicits a symbolic gift which is quite often placed in the body. Stein-brecher gives the following examples: an apple in the heart, a stick of green wood in the right hand, pearls around the neck. Such gifts clearly represent both outer and inner qualities. If employing this system it would be important to integrate and apply each gift in turn before seeking another.

Here is a very practical approach to the unconscious and to personal growth. Having met the Inner Guide we may seek dialogue with the Tarot figures. Each character can act as an inner teacher. We may take the most mundane and practical difficulties of every day life into this inner reality. Each character may be thought of as a specialist in a partic-ular area of experience Steinbrecher suggests translating the natal horo-scope into its Tarot equivalent as a means of structuring our encounters. There is sense in organizing a programme of inner work according to the strengths and weaknesses revealed through the chart. On the other hand, we may want to seek inner advice on a more ad hoc basis in which case we need to know to whom we should direct our questions. If seeking advice from the dynamic Tarot Trumps, go through the meditation of the guide. Do not be surprised if the characters you meet do not always resemble the Tarot Trumps with which you are familiar. The Devil may appear as a businessman, the World may appear as an astronaut.

The Inner Council of Wisdom

The Fool – Matters of spiritual direction and long term direction.
The Magician – Matters of action and the proper use of will.
The High Priestess – Matters of reflection and introspection.
The Empress – Matters of fertility and motherhood.
The Emperor – Matters of organization and structure.
The Hierophant – Matters of religion.
The Lovers – Matters of relationships.
The Chariot – Matters of achievement and success.
Strength – Matters of trial and personal test.
The Hermit – Matters of solitary development.
The Wheel – Matters of cyclic change.
Justice – Matters of law.
The Hanged Man – Matters of personal sacrifice.
Death – Matters of transformation.
Temperance – Matters of balance.
The Devil – Matters of temptation.
The Tower – Matters of downfall.
The Star – Matters of grace.
The Moon – Matters of the unconscious.
The Sun – Matters of joy.
Judgement – Matters of choice.
The World – Matters of mundane significance.

I used The Inner Guide meditation myself many years ago. At the time I was quite surprised by its powerful impact. I did encounter an Inner Guide. According to instruction, I also asked to see the Sun in human form. I remember well how surprised I was to find myself instantly transported to a walled garden in a desert landscape where I met my Sun in the guise of a gardener – an appropriate presentation for one who tended the garden of my being. I visited several Trumps under the direction of the Guide and found all encounters enlightening. On one occasion I asked to meet the High Priestess and was surprised to find her in the kitchen scrubbing pans. Our interchange served to show me that even the highest Wisdom has to be connected to daily life.

EXERCISE 37

Perform the Inner Guide meditation.

If we wish to adopt a systematic approach to the inner dynamics of the Tarot, we may follow Steinbrecher's advice and translate the personal horoscope into Tarot imagery. In this way it becomes possible to explore the natal chart through an inner dialogue with the Tarot Trumps. This system translates the planets into Tarot Trumps. Dialogue and interaction with these personified forces is quite straightforward. In the presence of the Inner Guide invite the Trumps speaking as the aspects to enter into dialogue. The approach can provide insight and guidance.

The chart is translated into Tarot form using the following guidelines.

Uranus	The Fool	Libra	Justice
Mercury	The Magician	Neptune	The Hanged Man
Moon	The High Priestess	Scorpio	Death
Venus	The Empress	Sagittarius	Temperance
Aries	The Emperor	Capricorn	The Devil
Taurus	The Hierophant	Mars	The Tower
Gemini	The Lovers	Aquarius	The Star
Cancer	The Chariot	Pisces	The Moon
Leo	Strength	Sun	The Sun
Virgo	The Hermit	Pluto	Judgement
Jupiter	The Wheel of Fortune	Saturn	The World

The aspects are approached in the following way:

1. The High Energy Relationships – aspects offering the most strength

'Ask them what they need from each other to begin working together within you as energies in harmony.' Look for:

Squares 90°
Oppositions 180°
The sign on the Ascendant and its opposite
The sign that the Sun is in and its opposite

The sign that the Moon is in and its opposite
The sign of the Midheaven and its opposite
Cancer – Capricorn polarity
Aries – Libra polarity

2. The Unions – energies that should be working together

'Ask what they need from each other and from your life.' Look for:

Conjunctions 0°
Sextiles 60°
Quincunxes 150°
Quintiles 72°

3. The Basic Archetypes – final dispositors of the horoscope

'Treat these with the addition of your guide as a "board of advisers".' Look
for:

The Sun and its sign
Ruler of the Ascendant and its sign
Any planets in their own rulership, or mutual reception

4. The Circles of Hands – three or more planets that connect to one another

'Form a circle of hands including your guide, ask the entire group
what you can do or stop doing to allow them to remain in balance.' Look
for:

Cardinal, Fixed, Mutable & Grand Crosses
T. Cross, Grand Trine, The Grand Square, The Yod Cross

5. The Specialized Constructs

The Function of the High Priest
Sun conjunct Saturn, Uranus, Neptune or Pluto

The Function of the High Priestess
Moon conjunct Saturn, Uranus, Neptune or Pluto

The Energy Receivers and Broadcasters
Saturn, Uranus, Neptune or Pluto in first house or conjunct the Ascendant

6. The Resistant Factors

'Ask the two energies to combine into a third which represents both figures containing the energy of both.' Look for:

Planets in detriment or fall in men
Planets in their exaltation or rulership in women
Planets in seventh and twelfth house

EXERCISE 38

If possible set up your own horoscope and translate it into Tarot terms.

Steinbrecher's approach has value. It presents a simple and effective means of interacting with the Tarot Trumps. His system expands the intuition and demonstrates the intimate connection between outer and inner realities. However, the natal chart cannot fulfil a truly initiatory function, we must look beyond it to a universal model such as the Tree of Life.

The Tarot in combination with the Tree of Life presents an initiatory structure. This simply means that as we integrate the experiences represented by both Tarot and Qabalistic symbols, we are changed. Our attitudes, beliefs and understanding are changed, our consciousness expands. We need to work through with the Trumps in order of ascent not descent. Students are often surprised to discover that when we follow the path of The Serpent of Wisdom, we commence with Trump XXI. The initiatory process must begin in the circumstances and limitations of everyday life. In other words we set out from the physical environment represented by the Trump, the World and aspire to travel towards the realms represented by Trump 0, the Spirit of Aethyr. Our initiatory path then is as follows:

The Path of the Serpent of Wisdom

Tarot Trump XXI, The World
Tarot Trump XX, Judgement
Tarot Trump XIX, The Sun
Tarot Trump XVIII, The Moon
Tarot Trump XVII, The Star
Tarot Trump XVI, The Tower
Tarot Trump XV, The Devil
Tarot Trump XIV, Temperance
Tarot Trump XIII, Death
Tarot Trump XII, The Hanged Man
Tarot Trump XI, Justice
Tarot Trump X, The Wheel
Tarot Trump IX, The Hermit
Tarot Trump VIII, Strength
Tarot Trump VII, The Chariot
Tarot Trump VI, The Lovers
Tarot Trump V, The Hierophant
Tarot Trump IV, The Emperor
Tarot Trump III, The Empress
Tarot Trump II, The High Priestess
Tarot Trump I, The Magician
Tarot Trump 0, The Fool

CHAPTER SIX

Stages and Paths

*The merely academic study of magical symbolism may be likened to
the analysis of musical scores by a student who does not know that
the documents he meticulously annotates are merely indications for
the evocation of music from instruments of whose very existence he
is ignorant.*
Paul Foster Case

Qabalah was originally an oral tradition passed from teacher to student.
The word Qabalah is derived from Qbl, *qibel* meaning 'to receive'. It has
been called 'The Yoga of the West'. We are all now familiar with Yoga.
We are less familiar with Qabalah.

Qabalah is a philosophy, a practice and a Path, a spiritual tradition, a
map of realities great and small, an initiation system and more besides. Its
origins are obscure. Legend states that it was received by Abraham, the
father of the Jewish nation. Emerging from a persecuted people, the
Qabalah has always been shrouded within an aura of secrecy, a protective
shield.

The transmission of teachings has been preserved not through books
which may always be destroyed, nor exclusively through a lineage of
teachers but through a single but complex image, the Otz Chum, The
Tree of Life. The Wheel of Life originated within the esoteric face of
Buddhism. The Tree of Life originated within esoteric Judaism.

We may regard the Tree of Life as a symbolic code. We may unlock this
code if we apply the correct keys. The Tarot Trumps provide one important set of keys.

To understand how the Tarot Trumps relate to the Tree of Life, we
have to become acquainted with the basic structure of the Tree itself. It
may appear that we are complicating our study of Tarot by introducing
another complete and complex symbol system. The Tree of Life does
not have to be daunting. Even a basic understanding of the Tree will
immeasurably enrich our understanding of Tarot. Furthermore, it is the
interrelationship between the Tarot and the Tree which takes us directly

into the current of the Western Mysteries. Our labours will therefore not be in vain.

The Structure Of The Tree Of Life

In thirty-two mysterious paths of wisdom did God decree – the God of Hosts, the Living God and King of the Universe, the Almighty God, Merciful and Gracious, High and Exalted, dwelling aloft eternally. Holy in His Name. He created His universe with three numerations: Number, Speech and Writing.
Sepher Yetzirah, Chapter I

The Tree of life is divided into thirty-two Paths and ten Sephiroth, 'emanations'. 'Ten not nine, ten and not eleven' says the *Sepher Yetzirah*. The Sephiroth are numbered 1–10. The Paths are numbered 11–32. Additionally, however, there is an eleventh sphere, Daath which is not regarded as a full Sephirah. This is the structure of our map.

The Sephiroth represent states of consciousness. They are emanations of the divine consciousness. Chapter 1 of the *Sepher Yetzirah* reminds us

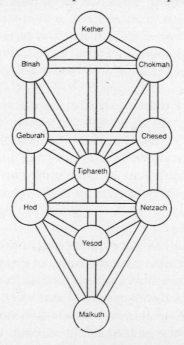

Fig. 14. The Sephiroth on the Tree of Life

of the nature of the Sephiroth. 'The ten ineffable Sephiroth have ten vast regions bound unto them; boundless in origin and having no ending; an abyss of good and ill, measureless height and depth; boundless to the East and the West; boundless to the North and the South and the Lord the only God, the Faithful King rules all these from his holy seat for ever and ever.'[1]

The Sephiroth are as follows:

1. Kether – The Crown
2. Chokmah – Wisdom
3. Binah – Understanding
4. Geburah – (Pachad) Severity
5. Chesed – (Gedulah) Mercy

6. Tiphareth – Beauty
7. Hod – Splendour
8. Netzach – Victory
9. Yesod – The Foundation
10. Malkuth – The Kingdom

EXERCISE 39
Become familiar with the names and positions of the Sephiroth.

The ten Sephiroth together create a multi-dimensional map. Each Sephirah is itself a region, a domain, a part of the whole map. As we become familiar with its territory, we become familiar with ourselves. Each Sephirah portrays both macrocosmic and microcosmic realities. 'As Above so Below', states the Hermetic maxim. The nature of each Sephirah is portrayed through its title. For instance, Malkuth, the Kingdom, symbolizes the physical world in which we live. It is our communal kingdom. It is the land, the planet itself. The dynamic function of each Sephirah is presented through its spiritual experience. These are the turning points of the soul. They are integrated into the personal psyche through varied inner work. Each Sephirah presents both a Vice and a Virtue. This polarity represents the positive and negative response to the nature of the Sephirah. There are additionally many other attributions and connected symbols which are of more relevance to the Qabalah student.

We have already seen how symbols have the power to both reflect and change consciousness. Here is a symbol system par excellence. We do not encounter single symbols but constellations of powerfully interconnected images. We do not encounter isolated symbols but move through layer after layer of symbolic mind-language. We are taken into the unconscious, immersed in symbolic images and then returned to the bright light of consciousness when we may examine the treasures we have discovered on the journey.

The Sephiroth are connected by twenty-two Paths which are also called stages or grades. Like the Sephiroth these too are accorded a number of attributions which reveal the function of the individual Path. Each Path is assigned a Tarot Trump. This symbolizes the subjective experience which connects two Sephiroth. In other words, it represents the experience which we need to undergo in order to shift our level of consciousness from that represented by one Sephirah to that represented by another. We may think of the Tree of Life as a building, a house or even a castle. Its rooms are the Sephiroth. Its corridors are the Paths. If we wish to travel from one room to another we make our way along the relevant corridors. The figures of the Tarot Trumps serve as guides, one allocated to each corridor. Corridors in great houses are never empty. We too will find an extraordinary wealth of additional symbols as we travel from one room to another. We will spend time absorbing their relevance too. Each Path or corridor is assigned a Hebrew letter. This is a key to the nature of the Path. Each Path is further assigned an astrological sign. This symbolizes the spiritual significance of the Path. We may like to classify the Sephiroth in the light of this analogy. The following is merely one suggestion. The student is free to create a personal list.

Room 10   The Chamber of the Earth
Room 9   The Chamber of Dreams
Room 8   The Chamber of Art
Room 7   The Chamber of Science
Room 6   The Chamber of Rebirth
Room 5   The Chamber of Purging
Room 4   The Chamber of Service
Room 3   The Chamber of the Great Mother
Room 2   The Chamber of the Great Father
Room 1   The Chamber of Sacred Wonders

We will examine the relationship between the twenty-two Trumps and the twenty-two Paths in more detail.

EXERCISE 40

Become familiar with the numbers of the Paths.

The Tree has three Pillars, The Pillar of Severity, The Pillar of Mercy and the Middle Pillar of Equilibrium or Consciousness. Furthermore, the Tree is divided into three Triangles of related energies. These represent

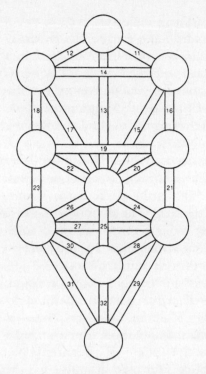

Fig. 15. The Paths of the Tree of Life

united states of consciousness composed of several Sephiroth together. The Supernal or Archetypal Triangle is composed of Kether, Chokmah and Binah. These together represent states of being far beyond the familiar. The subatomic particle dance is unfamiliar to us, yet it underpins the structure of the world in which we feel at home. The Moral or Ethical Triangle is composed of Chesed, Geburah and Tiphareth. Together these three Sephiroth initiate the individual into particular modes of consciousness which place Self at the service of the whole. The Astral or Psychological Triangle is composed of Malkuth, Hod and Netzach. These three Sephiroth initiate into balanced emotional and mental responses. Work within this Triangle modifies the personality, preparing it to become the channel for higher modes of consciousness to manifest. Travel between the Sephiroth, between the different levels of being is accomplished with the assistance of Tarot symbolism.

The triangular division of the Tree enables us to make coherent sense of varied experiences. In a similar way the Tree is also divided into four levels or Worlds of Being. The Archetypal World or Atziluth is composed solely by Kether, the Crown. The human mind cannot touch this level except through its reflected image at lower levels. The Creative World, Briah is composed of Chokmah and Binah. The Formative World, Yetzirah is composed of Chesed, Geburah, Tiphareth, Hod, Netzach and Yesod. The Material World, Assiah consists of Malkuth alone. This fourfold structure is a vital key. It tells us that what we perceive as matter is in fact the end result of a process of concretion. Matter is an effect, not a cause in itself. If we wish to create change at a physical level we have to work from the spiritual planes downwards.

These distinctions and divisions within the Tree are eminently practical. When we unfold a map and look up our destination, we next search for a grid reference. This enables us to narrow our focus and concentrate on a single area of the map. The divisions of the Tree serve in effect as grid references. First, we have to specify our destination. For instance, let us assume that we have identified an imbalance within ourselves. We recognize an instability in our emotional response. We respond too quickly from the heart and fail to evaluate decisions properly. We can see that our problem is related to what is called the Astral or Psychological Triangle. This covers Malkuth, Hod and Netzach. Malkuth represents the world of physical manifestation which includes our physical make-up. Hod represents the sphere of the mind. Netzach represents the sphere of the emotions. Our own diagnosis has shown us that we draw too readily upon the emotions and do not sufficiently use the powers of the mind represented by Hod. When we examine the Tree we find that if we are to travel from Malkuth to Hod, we encounter Tarot Trump XX; fittingly enough it is called Judgement, the very quality we are seeking to foster within ourselves. Furthermore, if we examine the path between Hod and Netzach we find the Tarot Trump XVI, the Tower. This Trump portrays the restructuring of the personality, the very process that we seek. Meditation upon the relevant Trumps will help us develop the qualities that we have identified. The same principles apply throughout the Tree. It is truly a map of our being.

EXERCISE 41
Meditate on the Four Worlds.

'The Tarot, the most satisfactory of all systems of divination, rises from and finds explanation in the Tree and nowhere else' (Dion Fortune).

We can already sense the complexity and indeed flexibility of the Tree. We can use its structure to contemplate polarities, trinities and quarternities.

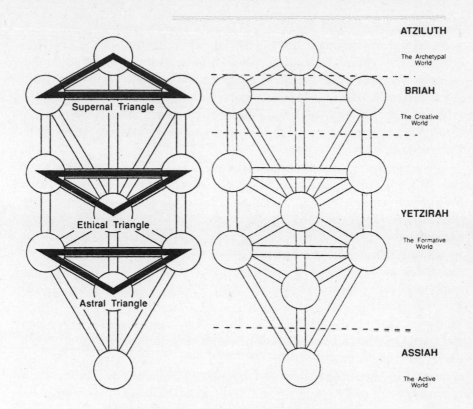

Fig. 16 The Triangles on the Tree of Life
Fig. 17 The Tree of Life and the Four Worlds

We can symbolically relate the physical world represented by Malkuth with the divine source represented by Kether. The Tree enables us to contemplate the human and the divine, it enables us to envisage the journey between the material and the non-material. It enables us to tread the Path by living out the relationships presented through the Tree.

We can now see that the Tarot Trumps correspond to particular spiritual stages, if we take the Tree as our blueprint. We grow beyond personality into individuality and finally mature as a spiritual being. It is too easy to elevate the personality, inflate the ego and mistake the reality of the physical body for the only reality. These are after all the messages that society offers. However, Qabalah offers an alternative view of personality, ego and body. It presents a blueprint for the whole being, for the immortal traveller journeying through time. The blueprint is accessible. You are ever invited to explore its twenty-two Paths.

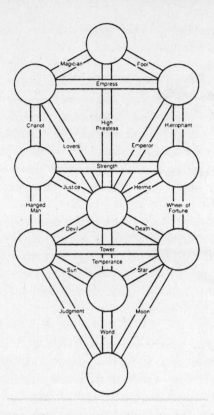

Fig. 18. The Tarot Trumps on the Tree of Life

EXERCISE 42

What areas of the Tree would assist you to develop dream recall, analytical thinking and the quality of service? Identify the relevant Sephiroth and Tarot Trumps.

Exploration is a matter of personal discovery and active involvement. This is most definitely not an intellectual pursuit. Robert Wang expresses this very clearly.

The problem arises in that to study any aspect of the Mysteries the investigator must himself become a part of the system. He must evaluate it from the inside, which may make it appear that he has abrogated investigative objectivity. Today's academicism does not allow for the acquisition of knowledge through intuition and psychism, an attitude placing it in paradoxical contradiction

to a high proportion of those great thinkers whom the Hum-
anities study and purport to revere.[2]

Exploration alone brings the Tree to life. It is only active and intimate
involvement that initiates. Personal discovery brings a flexibility and freedom that is not obvious in the apparently rigid intellectual structure.
Gareth Knight, an intrepid inner traveller, has constantly demonstrated
that the Tree offers as much flexibility as the operator can tolerate. 'From a
formal Qabalistic point of view it was found possible to start any Path
working from virtually any Tarot Trump – which suggests that the sacro-
sanct and rigid application of Tarot correspondences to the Tree of Life
is of little real importance.'[3] This boldness is not welcome in more traditional quarters. However, we have to be confident and competent in deal-
ing with inner dynamics before we attempt the revolutionary. In *A Practical
Guide to Qabalistic Symbolism* Gareth Knight offers a schema of being
according to the Tarot and the Tree. The student will note that this does
not follow the numerical order.

> The gateway of the Path to be worked should be visualized in the
> appropriate position and across the gateway the appropriate Tarot
> Trump as if painted on a curtain or a veil. After an invocation of
> the Divine Name and the Archangel of the Sephirah, one app-
> roaches the picture of the Tarot Trump. As one approaches it should
> take on a three-dimensional appearance and one then walks upon
> the Path and any images that arise spontaneously in consciousness
> should be noted. In order to keep one's bearings there are two main
> identification marks or sign posts along the path. At the mid-point
> of the Path is the Hebrew letter which can be visualized in white
> light or in the appropriate colour; while at the far end of the Path is
> the astrological sign, visualized similarly, and the environs of the
> further Sephirah.[4]

As the student travels from Temple to Temple, Sephirah to Sephirah via
the Paths so the experience of both is incorporated and integrated. The
essence of this work is to make the images live, to vivify them within
the psyche. Diagrams and models are useful guides, no more than that.
The real work is done within.

The Tree of Life is still worked in this way. The entire structure of the
Tree, both Sephiroth and Paths are experienced and internalized. The
following contemporary example shows how Tarot imagery is brought
to life as part of a series of Qabalistic Path-workings.

Awareness of our normal surroundings slips away gradually and in its place the Temple of Malkuth grows around us. It is square in shape with a floor of black and white tiles that feel cool to our sandalled feet. The north wall is on our left, the west behind us, the south to our right. Set into these three walls are circular windows of richly stained glass each a representation of a Holy Creature of that quarter. In the north it is a winged Bull, set in a circle of golden wheat and scarlet poppies. Behind us in the west, an Eagle soars into the sun through a sky of brilliant blue. In the south a winged Lion stands guard surrounded by flames. [The traveller encounters the archangel Sandalphon and finally pre-pares to leave the Temple.] Over the door forms a curtain depicting the Tarot card of the World. It glows brighter, then becomes a three dimensional door to the thirty-second Path. We walk between the pillars, the dancer hangs motionless within her wreath of leaves as we step forward into a swirl of Colour.[5]

The meditation continues as the traveller passes through the curtain to experience the inner realities which lie between the physical world and its etheric substratum. According to Melita Denning and Osborne Phillips, the rewards of this Path are 'the psyche's consciousness of liberation from the weight of material existence'. The technique of applied creative

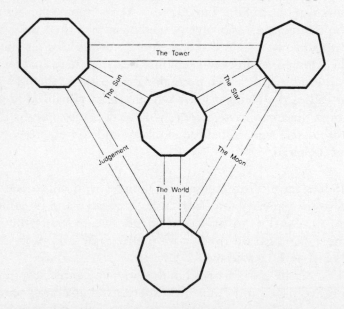

Fig. 19. Temples and Paths of the Astral and Material Worlds

imagination is deceptively simple to describe. In reality, however, the technique is hard to master and not without its pitfalls.

We can see from this short extract how relevant symbols are brought to life through the active imagination. If we are not already intellectually acquainted with the symbols, the images will simply fall flat in the mind and fail to serve any inner purpose.

The Tree of Life offers a vast complex of interconnected symbols which have to be individually vivified. The symbols whether strictly Qabalistic or Tarot are brought to life through the same process: intellectual study, intuitive exploration and internalisation. This is clearly a long term organic process, which cannot be hurried. It can take several years before the individual is transformed. Initiation is an active process of continuous inner change. It can only be accomplished through positive integration. Each single integration brings an extraordinary expansion of consciousness. The massive absorption represented by the full range of Tarot imagery brings total change. Through time and teaching the individual is transformed from the fragmented, personality-based expression of being to a complete and unified being, an image of the Tree in accordance with the axiom, 'As Above so Below'.

CHAPTER SEVEN

Initiation and Individuation

Every one of the Keys corresponds to something in your own make—up.
Paul Foster Case

We have defined initiation simply as a beginning. It marks the crossing of a threshold. It is a dividing line of significance. Initiations can be both great and small. An initiatory experience is one which precipitates a personal realization. We have realizations about ourselves all the time as part of daily life. We may realize that we are in the wrong career, that we must make an effort to call an old friend, that we must try to repair a relationship. The difference between those realizations which arise spontaneously and those which arise directly as a result of immersion in spiritual work remains one of intent and pace. Rather than let the circumstances of life initiate us in a haphazard and random fashion, we undertake the work of our own growth with intent. In this way we take responsibility for ourselves at all levels of being.

Who can deny the complexity and depth of the human psyche? We are all surely seeking answers to important life questions. We need to understand ourselves as fully as possible. Upbringing, early influences, parents and friends all have a part to play in the way we behave and react. Grief, loss, trauma, joy, success and achievement all influence the ways in which we think and feel. We are deeply and profoundly affected by the past. Self-knowledge is often difficult when we are gripped unconsciously by events long forgotten. Yet if we cannot gain self-knowledge, we can never be free from the tyranny of the past. We must hold up the mirror to the self, so that we may observe our own reflections with some objectivity. This of course is essentially the task of the therapist, the counsellor or the psychiatrist. In many senses, a living spiritual tradition both fulfils and surpasses the function of the counsellor as it takes the individual beyond the confines of the personality into transpersonal realms.

Know Thyself

In our ordinary life we are limited and bound in a thousand ways – the
prey of illusions and phantasms, the slaves of unrecognised complexes,
tossed hither and thither by external influences. blinded, and hypnotised
by deceiving appearances.
Robert Assagioli

All personal introspection whether under the guidance of a therapist
or within the discipline of a spiritual tradition seeks to answer a simple
question, namely, 'Know Thyself'. The question is deceptively simple, the
answer is extremely complex. When we return to this question over
and over again, we precipitate insight. The Tarot gives birth to insight. It
awakens our intuition by presenting questions in non-verbal form. If each
card merely presented us with a long list of questions, we would not be as
stretched as we are. For we have both to discover the questions and formulate the answer for ourselves. The rational mind is a skilled manipulator
of events both past and present as any therapist knows. The deductive
mind justifies and rationalizes. It provides reasons and offers explanations.
It is consummate at hiding personal truth. Rational answers to rational
questions rarely serve the cause of self-knowledge. If we truly seek to
know ourselves we must examine motives, aspirations and our hidden
feelings. To do this we must be prepared to ask a deeper level of consciousness. The Tarot speaks directly to the unconscious mind. The Tarot holds
up the mirror to the self. It will help us to discover who we are.

MAPS OF THE SELF

There are many models of the self which may serve us as we seek insight
into ourselves. Each model may have something to teach us. Indeed we
may find an extraordinary degree of harmony between seemingly different models. The Tarot combined with the Tree of Life offers an extra-
ordinarily rich model of the self. These models are maps of the psyche.
Each will help us to negotiate a part of our personal journey. Inner
maps, unlike outer ones, can only be integrated slowly. We have to travel
each part of it to understand its true significance for us.

Every step which enables us to move forward is won through an inner
realization. Every junction which takes us to a new road is won through a
specifically important realization, an initiation. We may understand the

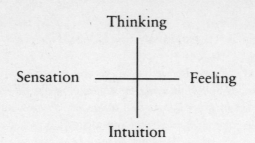

Fig. 20. The Four Functions

power inherent within a complex model such as the Tree by starting with
a very straightforward one: Jung's simple but effective analysis of the four
functions remains an excellent starting point for personal reflection.

According to the model we will each have a superior function which
we naturally draw upon and an inferior function which we rarely use. This
simple map enables us instantly to look within ourselves so that we may
discover how we employ these functions in daily life.

EXERCISE 43 – THE FOUR FUNCTIONS

Find out how you relate to these four functions. If the answer is
not obvious, observe your behaviour and interactions on a daily
basis. Become aware of the ways in which you naturally relate to
people and events. Do you rationalize or empathize? Do you
depend on your senses or your sixth sense? When you have become
familiar with your natural *modus operandi*, place all four functions in
the order in which you use them.

The Four Suits

These four functions correspond to the four suits of the Tarot.

1.   The Function of Thinking   The Suit of Swords
2.   The Function of Feeling   The Suit of Cups
3.   The Function of Intuition   The Suit of Wands
4.   The Function of Sensation   The Suit of Discs

EXERCISE 44 – SUITS AND SYMBOLS

In what way do the symbols assigned to the suits suggest their psychological functions?

We can pursue this simple analysis further and turn it to our distinct advantage in ordinary life. These functions represent our most immediate means of relating to the events of daily life. Each function has its own strengths and weaknesses. If we use thinking as our primary function, we will devalue feeling. As individuals we may have trouble relating to others. We may be uncomfortable in situations which require inspired guesswork. We may be exasperated by others who react primarily from an emotional level. We may be overly detached and cold.

If feeling is our primary function, we will feel threatened by cold analysis. We will dislike having to provide rational explanations. We are good at listening to others and have a natural rapport. However, we have a sneaking suspicion about anyone who doesn't operate from the heart too.

If intuition is our natural function, we fly upon hunches which are most often right. This can infuriate others who demand to know how we arrive spontaneously at decisions. We dislike the pedantry of analysis and distrust the instability of the emotions. We find it hard to put up with plodders and those who do not appreciate inspiration.

If sensation is our primary function, we will depend upon our senses for sound advice. We are distrustful of whims and hunches. We feel threatened by visionaries and dreamers. We feel safest with our feet on the ground. We like to be sure before we make decisions.

When we recognize ourselves, we are better prepared to understand the ordinary events of daily life at both home and at work. We may make allowances for others instead of just being exasperated by a personality clash. We may even begin to modify our behaviour in the light of this self-knowledge. A personal realization may lead directly to a new course of action. We may feel that our own imbalance between the four functions is itself a problem as we are provided with an unchanging means of reacting. We may feel that it could be valuable to strengthen the weaker of these functions. Jung merely provided the schema, he did not offer solutions. However dynamic psychology assumes:

1. That personal growth is possible.
2. That personal growth is important.
3. That growth takes places in response to particular triggers whether real or imagined.

For example, we may recognize that we have difficulties in expressing our feelings. This is preventing us from making friends and developing relationships. We recognize that we need to make a new beginning into the emotional life. We may refer to this as our need to experience an initiation into the function of feeling. This is symbolized by the element of Water. In life a painful love affair is the classic initiator. In the same way we may recognize that we are weak in the element of Fire, Air or Earth, the functions of thinking, intuition or sensation.

Initiation – A New Beginning

A technique can be regarded as a specific psychological procedure used in order to produce a definite effect on some aspect or on some function of the psyche.
Robert Assagioli

We may actively use the symbols of the Tarot to bring about a change for the better. We may take ourselves through initiation into these functions as represented by the elemental suits of the Tarot. In effect, we immerse ourselves in representations of the qualities we seek to develop. All work with the psyche should be undertaken seriously and with intent. We are in effect preparing to be midwives for we expect a birth within our own being. Life initiates us informally all the time. Self-initiation, however, takes place formally at a time of our choosing. We need first to clarify our intent. A simple way of doing this is to establish your aims. For instance in the present example, the personal goal might be as follows: 'I need to take the initiation into the element of Water and the function of feeling because I recognize that my emotional expression is blocked'. All such decisions which affirm the intention to precipitate a new beginning should always be impelled by a clear goal and sincere desire for personal growth.

Before we proceed we need to understand the principles involved. Paradoxically we may correctly define initiation as a beginning, but may also define it as an ending. For it represents the culmination of our initial decision to create change within ourselves. Initiation is both a beginning and ending, process and event. We may perceive the initiatory path as a cycle of continuous growth.

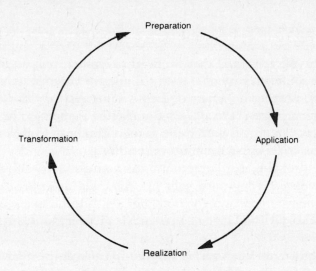

Fig. 21 The Cycle of Initiation

1. Preparation

In this period we make ourselves ready by meditating on the relevant symbols.

2. Application

This may be described in terms of a particular event. It is the trigger which we employ with both intent and care.

3. Realization

Realizations may take place within the event that we have undertaken to perform. It may not always appear in obvious form. It may come in the form of a feeling. A symbol may arise spontaneously in the mind. The realization may be deferred and may appear quite unexpectedly as a sudden thought popping into the mind or even through a dream. These realizations are often fleeting. It is important therefore to record all relevant thoughts, symbols and images as they arise. Realizations which take a symbolic form may require further meditation and reflection.

4. Transformation

When we have precipitated a series of realizations through the focus of our work, their cumulative weight serves to produce personal transformation and initiate growth. This aspect of the process is less easy to identify on a day-to-day basis. We tend not to see ourselves changing. Inner work of this kind acts like trigger within the psyche. You have made a beginning. You have placed a particular function within yourself under the microscope. Like dropping a stone into a pool, you can expect the ripples of your experience to flow into your life for some time. Personal change can sometimes be dramatic. Inner change tends to be mirrored in outer change, eating patterns, general activities and aspirations often reflect a new consciousness.

The following outline can be adapted to each of the elements. It can be understood as a psychological means of establishing a new beginning.

SELF-INITIATION INTO THE ELEMENTS AND THE PSYCHOLOGICAL FUNCTIONS

1. Preparation

Take the suit representing the function you wish to develop. Read all the meanings attributed to the suit. Meditate on them. Take the Court cards of the suit you are working with. Read the meanings attributed to these. Meditate on them and become familiar with the depiction of the Elemental Court so that you can see the characters with your eyes closed. Take as long as you require with this preparation. A week is suggested.

2. Application

EXERCISE 45

Undertake the following exercise. Set aside an uninterrupted period of time so that you can give it your full attention. Prepare a space and lay out the elemental cards 1–10 in a circle. Place the Court cards inside.

Find yourself standing in an antechamber within a castle. You wait. Ahead of you a pair of great double doors are closed. Beside the doorway you see a bell. You move forward and ring the bell. A deep note rings out. You stand back. The doors swing open slowly. You enter and find that you stand in a Great Hall. At the far end seated on a long low dais you see four crowned figures.

Here are the King, the Queen, the Prince and the Princess. An unseen voice rings out, 'Welcome to the Elemental Court'. You move forward further into the hall. A fanfare rings out. 'Let the Elemental Powers step forward.' Now from behind the dais a character dressed plainly comes to meet you. The character carries the Ace of the elemental suit and shows it to you. You meditate on it. The character returns. A new figure appears bearing the Two of the suit. In this way each character appears before you, bearing the appropriate Tarot card. The characters appear from the direction that you have prepared in your spread. When the bearer of the tenth card has returned, spend a few moments in quiet meditation before moving on to the next phase.

When you are ready, approach the dais where the Elemental Court sits.

Face the King and pose the question, 'What must I do to awaken the function of ...?'

Face the Queen and pose the question, 'What must I do to develop the function of ...?'

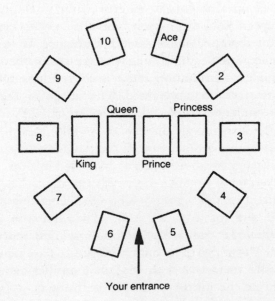

Fig. 22. The Elemental Court

Face the Prince and pose the question, 'What must I do to sustain the function of ...?'

Face the Princess and pose the question, 'What must I do to express the function of ...?'

Each question presents the opportunity for personal realization. Meditate on all that has transpired. Offer thanks for what has taken place. Close the meditation.

3. Realization

Write up your experiences straightaway.

4. Transformation

The work does not finish when the meditation closes. The impetus is transferred from the private interior experience into daily life and ordinary interaction. Become aware of the repercussions and effects of your work, recording the perceived results in your diary. These results may in turn become the subject for further reflection. The process becomes self-perpetuating. Initiation is a cycle.

When we set up a potentially transformative situation for ourselves we have no way of knowing how it will affect us. A certain degree of courage is required with all inner work. For instance, using the preceding example, an unexpected catharsis might take place in the following way. During the guided visualization there is a great upsurge of emotion when the Five of Cups is presented. The image of the cloaked and saddened figure suddenly evokes a distant memory. "A woman is being carried on a stretcher into an ambulance. A child cries in the arms of a father. The woman holds out a hand as she passes and says 'Don't worry.' The child is distraught with fear, already burdened by powerful emotions. Mummy is taken away because the child was angry. The child's anger was so great that it caused mummy to be sick." This long forgotten incident, repressed due to its power is now released into consciousness. The mature individual knows that mummy's sickness was not caused by childish anger. The old wound may now heal. This new insight may enable something to also heal in the adult mother-child relationship. When we hold up the mirror to the self with intent we should not be surprised when we see ourselves reflected in it.

Each of the Tarot suits may be used in the same way. We may safely explore and enrich these basic functions within ourselves. Do not hurry such work. It is important to allow all effects to be integrated into life. The four elemental initiations could be spread through the space of a year.

EXERCISE 46

Through meditation and introspection make your self-assessment. In what way would your ordinary life benefit from the strengthening of your weakest function? If you are ready to accept the responsibility for your own growth, undertake to perform an initiation into relevant element/function.

The Eternal Quest

Man's spiritual development is a long and arduous journey, an adventure through strange lands full of surprises, difficulties and even dangers. It involves drastic transmutation of the 'normal' elements of the personality, an awakening of potentialities hitherto dormant, a raising of consciousness to new realms and a functioning along a new inner dimension.
Robert Assagioli

All introspection and personal reflection is in reality the quest for self. The Tarot offers one model of the self. Qabalah offers another and indeed complementary model. Psychosynthesis offers another valuable model. It too can throw light onto our work with the Tarot. In common with all other spiritual models of the self, Psychosynthesis offers a model of wholeness and unity. Its thrust supports the premise, 'Know Thyself'. Wholeness is the goal of the work. It is accomplished through four stages.

1. A thorough knowledge of one's personality
2. The control of its various elements
3. The realization of one's true self – the discovery of a unifying centre
4. The formation or reconstruction of the personality around a unifying centre

We can see how these stages correspond to stages represented by the Tree of Life and attendant Tarot Trumps by setting the two systems together. We can also see how the Tree of Life extends a model of the self into transpersonal levels normally forgotten by purely psychological models. 'Psychosynthesis does not aim to give a metaphysical nor a theological explanation of the great mystery – it leads to the door but stops there.'[1]

1. Thorough Knowledge of One's Personality – The Paths of the Personality

The 32nd Path, Malkuth to Yesod, Tarot Trump XXI, The World
The 29th Path, Malkuth to Netzach, Tarot Trump XVIII, The Moon
The 31st Path, Malkuth to Hod, Tarot Trump XIX, The Sun

2. Control of its Various Elements – The Structure of the Personality

The 28th Path, Yesod to Netzach, Tarot Trump XVII, The Star
The 30th Path, Yesod to Hod, Tarot Trump XX, Judgement
The 27th Path, Hod to Netzach, Tarot Trump XVI, The Tower

3. Realization of One's True Self – The Discovery of a Unifying Centre – Links with Individuality

The 25th Path, Yesod to Tiphareth, Tarot Trump XIV, Temperance
The 26th Path, Hod to Tiphareth, Tarot Trump XV, The Devil
The 24th Path, Netzach to Tiphareth, Tarot Trump XIII, Death

4. The Formation or Reconstruction of the Personality around a Unifying Centre – The Structure of the Individuality

The Initiation of Tiphareth.

The Initiation of Tiphareth brings about a realignment of being. The personality surrenders to the Higher Self and becomes the servant instead of the master in the House of Self.

The Psychosynthesis Model

*Psychosynthesis can be applied by the individual himself or herself,
fostering and accelerating growth and self actualisation which should
be the aim of all and which is sometimes felt as an imperative inner
urge, as a vital existential necessity.*

Robert Assagioli

Psychosynthesis presents the following model:

1. *Lower Unconscious*

This contains the elementary psychological activities which direct the life
of the body. It includes all fundamental drives and urges. This is also the
seat of many emotional complexes, dreams and imaginations which are
allied to basic drives.

> The Sephiroth: Malkuth, Yesod, Netzach, Hod
> The Paths: 32nd (Malkuth to Yesod, Tarot Trump XXI, The World),
> 31st (Yesod to Hod, Tarot Trump XX, Judgement), 29th (Yesod to
> Netzach Tarot Trump, XVIII, The Moon)

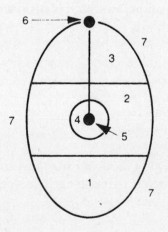

1. The Lower Unconscious
2. The Middle Unconscious
3. The Superconscious
4. The Field of Consciousness
5. The Conscious Self or 'I'
6. The Higher Self
7. The Collective Unconscious

Fig. 23. The Psychosynthesis Egg

2. The Middle Unconscious

This is where our various experiences are assimilated and the ordinary mental and imaginative activities are elaborated.

> The Sephiroth: Yesod, Netzach, Hod
> The Paths: 30th (Yesod to Hod, Tarot Trump XIX, The Sun), 28th (Yesod to Netzach, Tarot Trump XVII, The Star), 27th (Hod to Netzach, Tarot Trump XVI, The Tower)

3. Higher or Superconscious

> The Sephiroth: Tiphareth, Geburah, Chesed
> The Paths: 20th (Tiphareth to Chesed, Tarot Trump IX, The Hermit), 22nd (Tiphareth to Geburah, Tarot Trump XI, Justice), 19th (Geburah to Chesed, Tarot Trump VIII, Strength)

This contains our higher intuitions, inspirations, artistic, philosophical and ethical imperatives. It is also the source of altruism, genius and the centre for states such as contemplation, illumination and ecstasy.

4. The Field of Consciousness

This designates that part of the personality of which we are directly aware, the flow of sensations, thoughts, feelings, impulses which we can observe.

> The Sephirah: Malkuth

5. The Conscious Self or 'I'

> The Sephirah: Tiphareth

The conscious self emerges from the field of consciousness. It is an aspect of the Higher Self. It functions as a detached observer. It is sometimes referred to as the Watcher.

6. *The Higher Self*

The Sephirah: Tiphareth

The unifying centre is unlike the ego with which we normally identify ourselves. When we have discovered the unifying centre we may begin to align the personality to its powerful creative influence. The Higher Self is born through the Initiation of Tiphareth.

7. *The Collective Unconscious*

The collective unconscious is sometimes symbolized as a great sea. We are each part of this greater whole like individual cells in a body. If we use the term to describe the whole in which we are individual parts, we may use it to describe the Tree itself as a unit. The Psychosynthesis model uses the collective unconscious to describe the outer line seen in the diagram with the following proviso. 'The outer line of the diagram should be regarded as "delimiting" but not as "dividing". It should be regarded as analogous to a membrane delimiting a cell, which permits a constant and active interchange with the whole body to which the cell belongs.[2]

EXERCISE 47
What qualities of being do you ascribe to the Higher Self?
What qualities of being do you ascribe to the personality?

Psychosynthesis presents a model and a means for integration and self-realization. Tarot presents a model and means for integration and self-realization Qabalah presents a model and a means for integration and self-realization. The goal of the work is to become yourself, to individuate, which is the core process in analytical psychology. Finding the person one was always intended to be is both the process and the goal. Psychosynthesis actively recognizes that some people require 'a wider and higher type of Psychosynthesis, Spiritual Psychosynthesis'.[3] This admission acknowledges the fact that a fuller model permits greater individual growth. A purely psychological model is inadequate for those who have an inner need for transpersonal fulfilment. The Tree of Life together with integrated Tarot symbols offers a model which is both personal and transpersonal. Quite simply, Qabalah offers a greater map to the inner traveller. Assagioli states that 'what has been called by various people or thinkers, "spiritual" corresponds in great part to what can empirically be called the "superconscious".[4] In other words we may relate the superconscious with the reaches of Tree of Life above Tiphareth.

> The basic premise or hypothesis is that there exists – in addition to those parts of the unconscious which we have called the lower and middle unconscious, including the collective unconscious – another vast realm of our inner being which has been for the most part neglected by the science of psychology, although its nature and its human value are of a superior quality.[5]

We may therefore identify the superconscious as defined by Psychosynthesis with the transpersonal realms of the Tree of Life. Here we have not limited its field, but have used it as a foundation for even higher realizations and further transpersonal growth. We have defined the superconscious as the antechamber of the Supreme Mysteries. By this definition, the superconscious includes:

1. *The Greater Mysteries – The Structure of the Individuality*

The 20th Path, Tiphareth to Chesed, Tarot Trump IX, The Hermit
The 22nd Path, Tiphareth to Geburah, Tarot Trump XI, Justice
The 19th Path, Geburah to Chesed, Tarot Trump VIII, Strength

2. *Influences upon the Personality*

The 21st Path, Netzach to Chesed, Tarot Trump X, The Wheel
The 23rd Path, Netzach to Geburah, Tarot Trump XII, The Hanged Man

3. *The Links with the Spirit*

The 13th Path, Tiphareth to Kether, Tarot Trump II, The High Priestess
The 17th Path, Tiphareth to Binah, Tarot Trump VI, The Lovers
The 15th Path, Tiphareth to Chokmah, Tarot Trump IV, The Emperor

4. The Supreme Mysteries – The Paths of the Spirit

  The 18th Path, Geburah to Binah, Tarot Trump VII, The Chariot
  The 16th Path, Chesed to Chokmah, Tarot Trump V, The Hierophant

5. The Structure of the Spirit

  The 14th Path, Binah to Chokmah, Tarot Trump III, The Empress
  The 12th Path, Binah to Kether, Tarot Trump I, The Magician
  The 11th Path, Chokmah to Kether, Tarot Trump 0, The Fool

The images of the Tarot present an extraordinary opportunity for
transpersonal growth. Psychosynthesis offers techniques. Tarot offers the
relevant symbols. There is an extraordinary accord of approach. When
approaching the Tarot as a system for personal initiation, we bring the
symbols to life through creative visualization and internal dialogue.
Psychosynthesis offers exactly the same procedure as a means of awakening higher consciousness. It is suggested that when we seek spiritual
counsel we must seek the teacher within.

  It is necessary to make an inner journey, more exactly an ascent to
  the various levels of the conscious and superconscious psyche, to
  approach this inner teacher and then in the imagination to simply
  state the problem, talking to the imagined teacher realistically
  as if he were a living person and, as in everyday conversation
  courteously awaiting a response.[6]

This is exactly the method proposed through the Tarot Initiation. The
approach in many ways sounds too simple, too easy. It cannot be understood except through personal experience. The essence of the Tarot
Initiation lies in this approach.

  We also find further accord between the two systems. Assagioli describes the symbols which have the power to evoke the spiritual self.
We find the symbols for Spiritual Psychosynthesis, the highest reaches
of Assagioli's system deeply embedded in the Tarot. He describes two
main categories.

1. Abstract or Geometrical and Nature Symbols.

Sun
Star
Sphere of Fire
Rose or Lotus
Equilateral Triangle

2. Personified Symbols

An Angel
The Inner Christ
The Mystical Warrior
The Old Sage
Inner Teachers

When we look at these symbols in direct relation to the Tarot we find that they appear in various guises throughout the sequence of Trumps.

Sun – The Sun, Trump XIX
Star – The Star, Trump XVII
Sphere of Fire – The Element of Fire
Rose or Lotus – The Fool, Trump 0
Equilateral Triangle – Temperance, Trump XIV
Angel – Judgement, Trump XX, The Lovers, Trump VI, Temperance,
    Trump XV
The Inner Christ – The Hanged Man, Trump XII
Mystical Warrior – The Chariot, Trump VII
Old Sage – The Hermit, Trump IX
Inner Teachers – The Hierophant, Trump V, The Magician, Trump
    I, The High Priestess, Trump II.

The Tarot provides many more potent and evocative symbols. Its symbolic language is in fact incalculable, its value is beyond measure. For here are the very symbols which bring us to transcendence, the ultimate level of our being. As we come to understand how symbolic forms activate and transform psychic energy, our respect for the Wisdom of the Tarot can only grow. For we discover a subtle balance runs throughout the system. The four elemental suits which correspond to the fundamental functions, thinking, feeling, intuition and sensation, present a stable foundation for personal awakening. These functions form the bedrock of daily life. As we come to understand the four suits, we come to observe our own use of these basic functions. The Tarot presents another dynamic relationship for us, that between the conscious and unconscious mind. One is not sacrificed to the other. Solar symbols of consciousness, the light of reason exemplified by the Sun go hand in hand with lunar symbols which exemplify the hidden light of the subconscious. Male and female powers are balanced; Sun and Moon, Magician and High Priestess, Emperor and Empress, all elaborate the fundamental duality also expressed in the familiar Yin-Yang symbol. Yet this duality is always resolved. Polarity is resolved into unity through the Fool and the World, the Alpha and Omega of the sequence. The fourfold division is resolved by the fifth element Akasa, Spirit, ever present throughout the Trumps in a multitude of guises. These symbols of transcendence which succeed in balancing and containing natural opposites are of profound value to us. We each have to come to personal resolutions through the processes of our own development. The journey towards wholeness and integration has been called individuation, a 'process or course of development arising out of the conflict between two fundamental psychic facts'.[7]

The portrayal of dynamic opposites pinpoints the very heart of individuation whereby all oppositions find resolution. This process is not hard to observe for we should be able to see it, or indeed its absence, in everyone we meet. Imagine for a moment that you meet someone new. As you get to know them you come to discover what makes them tick. You find that your new acquaintance is extremely clever. In fact he likes to impress people with his general intellectual prowess. He has a very good memory and a wide range of knowledge. As you get to know him further, however, you begin to detect an emotional coldness. There is a lack of sympathy especially for those not naturally equipped with a good mind. You probe a little more deeply into your friend's inner life, perhaps by discussing dreams. You find that your friend rarely remembers dreams and attaches no importance to them whatsoever. You gradually come to see that your friend functions almost entirely through the function of thinking and the powers of the conscious mind. What you took to be an impressive intellect is in fact the over-development of one function at the expense of the others. Ask yourself, has this imaginary friend achieved a state of individuation? How will this person cope in a life crisis which cannot be solved through intellectual analysis?

Individuation

Individuation is the goal of life and the way one become truly ones self –
the person one was always intended to be.
Demarris S. Wehr

It was Jung who introduced the term individuation. He used it to refer
to the process by which a person becomes a psychological individual,
whole and complete in themselves. The term implies a level of maturity
and self-awareness, a coming into selfhood. Jung wrote of his own growing
comprehension of this process as he saw it at work in the lives of his
patients: 'Through the study of these collective transformation processes
and through understanding alchemical symbolism I arrived at the central
concept of my psychology: *the process of individuation*'.[8]

Until we have achieved individuation, we remain in the grip of the
personal ego and the mass group mind. We are ripe for exploitation by all
manipulators of group goals. We are easy prey for the media, advertising
and the image makers who pamper and further inflate the insatiable ego.
Individuation alone brings freedom from the tyranny of mass consciousness. Esther Harding, a Jungian therapist writes that 'One thing only can
stand against this power of the unconscious and paradoxical as it may
sound, is the power of individuality'.[9]

It is clear that not everyone becomes the person they were always
intended to be. In fact individuation is probably only uncommonly
achieved. Society itself frowns upon the unconventional. Creativity is
often perceived as a self-indulgent luxury. The quest for self is treated as
an eccentric aberration. Conformity is the goal of society which as a social
group, prefers regularity and compliance. Individuation, however, implies
no threat to the social order but rather releases the true human potential
and liberates creativity, vision and insight. By contrast social conformity
produces uniformity of outlook, limitation of perspective and acceptance
of material goals. Creativity fades, inspiration is stillborn. The individual
fails to become the person they were always intended to be. Instead, an
immature personality holding second-hand values attempts to fulfil all
accepted social and material obligations. The failure to live fully to this
pattern is seen repeatedly in the classic mid-life crisis. This appears when
all social and material obligations are fulfilled only to reveal a yawning gap
in personal meaning.

Society as a whole shows little interest in the findings of dynamic
psychology. Dynamic psychologists on the other hand are well aware that

their findings do have a relevance to society as a whole, for individual psychological well-being forms the single cell in the body politic. Assagioli discusses transmutation of the biological drives, especially the sexual and combative drives which, unchannelled, can be destructive. These same energies when directed and used for creative energies and achievement can instead become a force for personal growth. Assagioli sees application for Psychosynthesis in education, interpersonal relationships and general mental well-being. Society as a whole still fails to appreciate the value of psychological insight for the diverse individuals who make up the social unit. Individuated persons, whole in themselves, might just contribute more creatively and harmoniously to a greater whole, namely society.

EXERCISE 48

What do you understand by the term individuation?
What do you understand by the term initiation?

The Tarot And Individuation

Every symbol constitutes an intermediary.
Robert Assagioli

It is clear that the Tarot conveys the very images which are central to the process of individuation. It expresses the tension at the heart of the process in the battle between the unconscious and conscious. One might reasonably ask if all this is just a matter of becoming one's self why is it all so difficult. Why can't we just be as we are and allow life to take us where it wants? After all, life initiates. Why do we need complex models of the self? What is the imperative to undertake the Great Work, the journey into self? Jung himself posed the same question to his readers, 'Why cannot the unconscious be left to its own devices?'[10] He suggests that under certain cultural conditions no interference is required; the society provides its own balance of activities and outlets for both the conscious and the unconscious. However, Western culture provides no such balance and thereby creates its own problems. 'The psyche of civilized man is no longer a self-regulating system but could rather be compared to a machine whose speed regulation is so insensitive that it can continue to function to the point of self injury.'[11]

Our life currently offers few avenues for personal or spiritual growth. We have become trapped by materialistic goals. Religion has become a matter of morality. We have lost sight of spiritual goals. We live in a society which has replaced meaning with technology. Yet it is clear that neither technology nor materialism feed the inner human being. In the age of computers and video games, we are truly in danger of losing sight of the true source of our own growth, creativity and transcendence.

The process of individuation is impeded when appropriate spiritual nourishment is denied. We may balk at a reliance on psychological models to illustrate the human condition. Yet the prevailing cultural view of a person defined by career, status, income and assets is truly impoverished. If we hold an impoverished role model, we will create impoverished human beings. If we hold an enriched role model, we may create an enriched human being. We are in serious danger of presenting and believing in insubstantial, fragmented, flawed models which serve only to inflate the ego and produce spiritually starved zombies. The elevation of the rational mind has created an enormous cultural imbalance. The irrational elements within life are desperately hidden, controlled and sanitized. Yet we must walk the tightrope between thinking and feeling, analysis and meaning, creativity and deduction. We need psychological and spiritual models for human growth to remind us that not all can be accomplished through consumer goods and technological advance. We need Tarot to show us all that we are in danger of throwing away in our rush for progress. We need Tarot so that we may gaze into it and see our own reflections. Let us be dazzled at the complexity, depth and richness of what we find, for this is the human being. This is the Tarot Initiation.

CHAPTER EIGHT

Mandalas and Divinations

*It is not to be used for vulgar fortune telling, or to
amuse a party of friends.*
Paul Foster Case

Divination or 'reading the Tarot' is perhaps its most well known use. It is too often the only aspect of Tarot that is known. Divination is the mundane application of Tarot. There is much scope for misuse in this area by both readers and those who bring questions (querants). Over dependence on Tarot spreads does not foster spiritual growth. Slavish obedience to Tarot dictates does not bring liberation but another form of imprisonment. These words are not intended to diminish the use and value of Tarot divination but rather to preserve its proper exalted function, namely to serve as a mirror to the self.

Externalizing the interior process has great value. It is both cathartic and illuminating, bringing insight and releasing potential. Spontaneous drawing, free association and dreams each externalize the inner life. However, these personal expressions often provide yet another private language, compounding enigma with enigma. These mirrors of the self are idiosyncratic and personalized. A private language cannot be shared until it too is decoded. A shared language will translate deep inner processes into a code that can be directly read. This is Tarot, it is the translator of unconscious activity par excellence.

When we lay out the Tarot in the Spirit of Wisdom, we objectify the subjective, make the invisible visible and provide form for the formless. The Tarot exteriorizes the interior life, it reveals the inner life like disclosing fluid.

Mandalas – Mirrors to the Soul

Mandalas are birth places, vessels of birth in the most literal sense.
Carl G. Jung

The Tarot is not unique in its capacity to function as a reflecting mirror. Its strength, however, lies in its codified form. It speaks in a language that is readily accessible. It presents the archetypal powers in symbolic form, converting the powers of the unconscious into a form that the conscious mind recognizes.

Jung plunged headlong into his own interior life. His journey was, as he said, 'the prima materia' of his entire life. It took him deeply into the active exploration of symbolic forms. Through his own dynamic encounters, Jung came to recognize the significance of half-forgotten symbol-systems. He came to believe that alchemy, like Tarot, served as mirror to the soul; Its strange symbols representing interior processes of growth, death and transformation. His insights into alchemy led him to rediscover the power of the mandala, another mirror for the soul.

The rediscovery of this ancient form was important even in Jung's own growth; he had instinctively painted a mandala in 1916 but without understanding its significance. Some two years later the impulse to draw mandala forms returned. This time Jung experienced a conscious realization of their significance. 'In 1918–19 I sketched every morning in a notebook a small circular drawing, a mandala which seemed to correspond to my inner situation at the time. With the help of these drawings I could observe my psychic transformations from day to day.'[1] Jung had to rediscover what had never been lost in unbroken spiritual traditions. Tibetan Buddhism makes extensive use of the mandala form. The ceremonial Navajo sand paintings are mandalas. Hinduism has retained the sacred circle. The West had destroyed its own knowledge of sacred forms with the rise of an intellectually-based orthodoxy. Jung deepened his studies, explorations and discoveries. 'Only gradually did I discover what the mandala really is: "Formation, Transformation, Eternal Mind's eternal recreation". And that is the self, the wholeness of the personality.'[2]

Jung also observed the creation of mandalas in his therapeutic work with patients. He observed that the mandala served to express order, balance and wholeness at a time of disorientation or panic. In ordinary life it is at just such a time of crisis or decision-making that an individual might seek the help of a Tarot reader. A crisis destroys the old patterns; the querant is seeking to discover the new pattern.

Jung observed the creation of many mandalas as he worked with his patients over a period of time. He was able to group the symbols which emerged spontaneously in the healing process. When we look at these symbols we find an extraordinary accord with the images of Tarot.

1. *Circular, spherical or egg shaped formations:* decorations on the robe worn by the Fool, orb carried by the Emperor and Empress, the Wheel of Fortune, the Wreath surrounding the World Dancer.
2. *Flowers, especially the Rose or Lotus:* rose carried by the Fool, Lilies and Roses above and below the Magician, garland of flowers worn by Strength, banner carried by Death.
3. *A centre expressed by a sun or star:* the Sun, the Star.
4. *A fourfold structure:* a castle, city courtyard, temenos, circular or quadratic motifs Elemental weapons on the table of the Magician, the four Kerubs surrounding the Wheel, the four zodiacal creatures around the World, the city behind the Chariot and the fourfold symbolism of the Chariot.

He also included two further themes, Squaring the Circle, and the Eye. We do not find these symbols portrayed directly in the Rider–Waite pack. However, both these symbols are familiar to students of Tarot and esoteric tradition. Jung presents an example of a drawing by a young woman. It is rich in themes shared by the Tarot. He describes the painting thus:

> We see at the cardinal points four creatures a bird, a sheep, a snake and a lion with a human face. Together with the four colours in which the four regions are painted they embody the four principles … Animals generally signify the instinctive forces of the unconscious which are brought into unity within the mandala, this integration of the instincts is a prerequisite for individuation.[3]

We are reminded of the four zodiacal/elemental creatures in Tarot Trumps XXI and X, the World and the Wheel of Fortune.

We may draw upon the wisdom that Jung rediscovered and apply the same principles to the Tarot. The images of the Tarot may be combined with the form of the mandala to create the Tarot Mandala. Like Jung we may hold the mirror up to the self. In his mandalas Jung saw himself. 'My mandalas were cryptograms concerning the state of the self which were presented to me anew each day in them I saw the self that is my whole being actively at work.'[4] We too may draw upon the mandala so that we may glimpse the self.

The Tarot Mandala

The Spiritual Self is the greatest reality, the real essence of our being.
Robert Assagioli

Divination through the Tarot takes place through a spread, a layout of cards in a particular often symbolic arrangement. Each placement within the layout is accorded a significance. The divination coalesces as the meanings attributed to the individual cards, are read against the position in which they fall. Interrelationships between cards are also taken into consideration.

Using the Tarot as a mirror to the interior life is a matter for personal respect. Taken seriously and used wisely the Tarot Mandala can shed illumination into our lives. The following spreads each utilize a mandala form. It is suggested that only the Major Trumps should be used in conjunction with this spread. This is an unusual departure from normal divination practice. However, as we are seeking to understand the way in which the archetypal powers are personally experienced, we will look to the Major Arcana for our reflected picture. It is also common practice to attribute a 'reversed' meaning to a card should it fall upside down. This practice is not considered relevant to the Tarot Mandala. We will read all meanings from the positive non-reversed position.

DIVINATION 1 – WHO ARE YOU?

Establish your personal circle. You can do this as simply or as elaborately as you wish. Draw out a circle on a sheet of a paper or prepare and even decorate a piece of fabric to be reserved for your divinations.

Lay out your divination in the mandala. Enter an interior state of mind and formulate the question 'Who am I?' While dwelling on this, shuffle or cut the cards as you wish. When you are ready, take the card from the top of the deck and lay it in the centre of your circle. This will represent your Higher Self. Take the next card from the pack and lay it on top of the first Trump. This represents your personality. Note how the personality obscures the Higher Self from view. The central point of a mandala has a special significance. It is called the bindu point. Meditate on what is being presented to you. Record your divination in your diary.

Return to these Trumps in further meditations. Explore their meaning both intellectually and through your intuition. What do these two Trumps

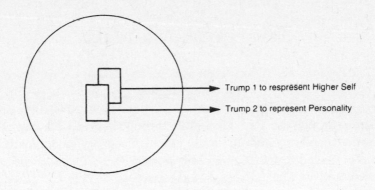

Fig. 24. Who Are You?

tell you about yourself? What light do these two Trumps throw on the relationship between the personality and the Higher Self? Your identification with both these Trumps may alter through time. You will intuitively know when this happens. Stay with the Trumps that come up in your first divination until you have totally internalized the significance of these two Trumps.

DIVINATION 2 – THE CYCLE OF BEING – THE OUTER CIRCLE

This divination represents your outer dynamic life which is shared with others. Refine your circle by including the four quarters. Do this literally, and by integrating the meanings attributed to the quarters. The circular form enables us to also attribute the quarters to the seasonal turning points of the year; the solstice and equinox landmarks. You now have four points of reference within the mandala.

1. *The East* The Point of Orientation The Element of Air The Function of Thinking The Spring Equinox.

The East represents beginnings, new activities, plans, ideas that you are generating.
    This placement represents those hopes and possibilities which exist only as visions and ideas in the mind.

2. *The South* The Point of Elaboration The Element of Fire The Function of Intuition The Summer Solstice.

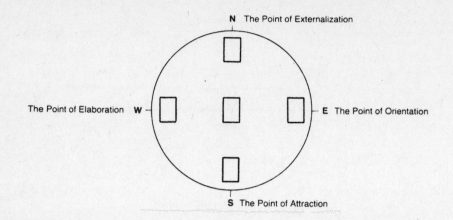

Fig. 25. The Cycle of Being

The South represents the way that a seed is nurtured into life with enthusiasms, interests, passion and commitment.

This placement represents the way in which we apply our energy to the task in hand.

3. *The West* The Point of Attraction The Element of Water The Function of Feeling The Autumn Equinox.

The West represents the way in which an interest brings new people, new acquaintances and introduces us to new networks.

This placement includes our relationships with others. It represents the vast potential generated by the emotional life.

4. *The North* The Point of Externalization The Element of Earth The Function of Sensation The Winter Solstice.

The North represents results, outcomes and the fruits of our labours.

This placement deals with endings and the material consequences of actions. The outcome represented here is never final in itself. One successfully-achieved goal acts a spur to new ideas and plans.

In the middle of your mandala, place the card which stands for your personality. Enter an interior state of mind and formulate the question. 'Show me the dynamics at work in my outer life.' Select out the card already indicated as representing your personality and place this at the centre. Shuffle or cut the cards as you wish. When you are ready, take the card from the top of the deck and lay it at the East. Take the next card and

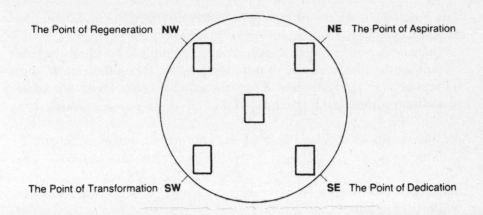

The Point of Regeneration **NW**   **NE** The Point of Aspiration

The Point of Transformation **SW**   **SE** The Point of Dedication

Fig. 26. The Cycle of Growth

lay it at the South. Lay the next two cards in the West and North respectively. Meditate on what is being presented to you.

What does this spread reveal about your outer life? Do you see any
relationship between the outer life and the personality as represented in
the divination? Record your divination in your diary.

DIVINATION – 3. THE CYCLE OF GROWTH – THE INNER CIRCLE.

This divination represents the interior life. We have talked about personal
and spiritual growth as being a continuous process. The process is never
static but ever-moving. A new value comes to birth, an old conception
fades, a realization gains strength, a breakthrough is close. This divination
uses the old Celtic year as its base. The four festivals of Imbolc, Beltane,
Lammas and Samhain form the reference points.

1. The North-East The Point of Aspiration Imbolc/Oimelc February 1 The
   Feast of Brighid.

The North-East placement represents your hopes, wishes, and plan for
your future inner growth.

This festival marks the lambing season. Its name means 'ewes milk'.
We can use this time to reflect on the inner seeds of our own growth.

2. The South-East The Point of Dedication Beltane April 30   Festival
   of May Eve.

The South-East placement represents your long-term commitment, the cause that you can believe in.

Beltane is a fire festival. It is a good time to light the fire within yourself, by fanning the flames of your consuming passion. This festival flows into traditional May Day activities of pageant and pole. May Day is the time to dedicate yourself to the fullness of life.

3. The South-West The Point of Transformation Lammas August 1
   The Harvest.

The South-West placement represents a place in your life where change will bring growth.

Lammas comes from the Old English Hlafmas meaning 'loaf mass'. Bread was made fresh from the harvest. It was a time of great celebration. As bread, the staff of life, is transformed from the grain, we too can reflect upon our own process of growth which is a continuous trans-formative flow.

4. The North-West   The Point of Regeneration   Samhain   November 1
   The Celtic New Year.

The North-West represents a place of rebirth.

It is the old Celtic New Year which marked the onset of winter. It was celebrated with traditional divination games. Our New Year resolutions are a resonance of this. The passing of the year is a good time for deep reflection and inner stock taking. We have to be prepared to prune that which is dead within ourselves so that the new may come to future birth.

In the middle of your mandala, place the Trump which stands for your Higher Self. Enter an interior state of mind and formulate the question. 'Show me the dynamics at work in my inner life.' Shuffle or cut the cards as you wish. When you are ready, take the card from the top of the deck and lay it at the North-East. Take the next card and lay it at the South-East. Lay the next two cards in the South-West and North-West respectively. Meditate on what is being presented to you. What do these two Trumps tell you about your inner life? Do you see any relationship between the inner life and the Higher Self as represented in the divination? Record your divination in your diary.

EXERCISE 48

   If you are not already familiar with these four festivals, read up on
   them.

We may make good use of the time reference represented in the mandala.
For instance suppose that Tarot Trump XV, the Devil, is laid at the Point
of Transformation indicating that we hold excessively material goals. We
might first reflect upon this statement and then choose to act in accordance with the principles previously indicated. We might plan a further
meditation as an act of conscious transformation. It might be possible
for this to coincide with the traditional celebration at that time of year.

DIVINATION 4 – THE PERSONAL CALENDAR

Use this divination to consciously plan a programme of work for a year.
You may work with either the inner or outer circle. Meditate on the
question, 'What inner/outer tasks should I undertake in this year?' As
before lay out your significator for the Higher Self/personality at the
centre. Lay out four Trumps as before. Use the time references as landmarks. Let us see how the following reading might help us to plan a year's
personal work.

THE CYCLE OF BEING – SAMPLE DIVINATION

1. In the East, The point of Orientation   The Emperor

Meaning: This Trump indicates a need for order. This placement indicates what you must look towards as a priority task. There is a great need
here to establish a smooth running and efficient structure. The message
here is 'Put your affairs in order'. This can be taken both literally and
metaphorically.

2. In the South, The Point of Elaboration   The Magician

Meaning: This Trump indicates the need for active involvement. This
placement indicates the way in which your daily life is lived. Clearly,
your mundane life is an expression of spiritual principle. Hold fast to
your beliefs and be confident that spiritual power is present even in the
most ordinary of tasks. The message here is, 'Throw all of your weight
into a cause in which you believe'.

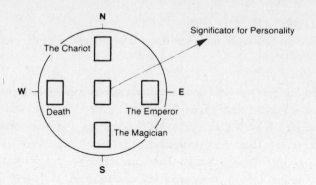

Fig. 27. The Cycle of Being – Sample Divination

3. In the West, The Point of Attraction   Death

Meaning: This Trump indicates that something will fall away. This place-ment indicates your relationship to significant others in your life. Be prepared for an upheaval or sudden change in the network in which you function. This will alter the power structure in which you and others function. The message here is, 'Be prepared for a process of transformation precipitated by loss'.

4. In the North, The Point of Externalization   The Chariot

Meaning: This Trump indicates a personal victory. This placement indicates the outcome and result of your outer orientation, ways of elaboration and powers of attraction. You will find success through an important role. You will be asked to use your authority and insight together to determine the direction of a particular group of people. The message here is, 'You will be asked to take full responsibility for shaping the future direction of a group to which you belong'.

THE CYCLE OF GROWTH – SAMPLE DIVINATION

1. In the North-East, The Point of Aspiration   Strength

Meaning: This Trump indicates the need for great personal resolve. Your aspirations will be put to the test, at times you will think of giving up. You will question your own fitness and inner strength. The message here is, 'You will stand alone, be prepared to be tested'.

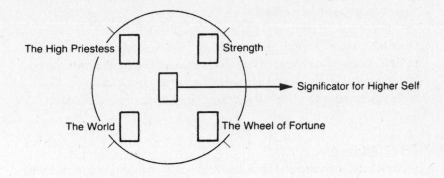

Fig. 28. The Cycle of Growth – Sample Divination

2. In the South-East, The Point of Dedication   The Wheel of Fortune

Meaning: This Trump indicates a new cycle coming into play. You will need move with new influences. Do not hold fixed views as to how your dedication may be realized. Hold on to your vision but allow its form of expression to be fluid. The message here is 'Your world will be turned upside down'.

3. In the South-West, The Point of Transformation   The World

Meaning: This Trump indicates big responsibilities. Your own process of inner transformation has taken you to a point where you are ready to actively assist in the transformation of others. This will involve new responsibilities both practical and spiritual. The message here is, 'Will you be ready to carry the task placed on your shoulders?'

4. In the North-West, The Point of Regeneration   The High Priestess

Meaning: This Trump indicates the importance of wisdom in our life. Your personal aspiration, dedication and transformation will be united through the function of wisdom and the inner service by identifying with the High Priestess. The message here is, 'Will you be ready to sit upon the Throne of Wisdom when you are asked?'

Let the themes of the divination become spiritual landmarks for the year. Use the themes indicated by the Tarot Trumps quite specifically in planning a personal calendar. Prepare meditations to coincide with the appropriate time of the year.

Using the preceding example:

At Imbolc take Strength as your theme for meditation.
At Beltane take the Wheel of Fortune as your theme for meditation.
At Lammas take the World as your theme for meditation.
At Samhain take the High Priestess your theme for meditation.

EXERCISE 49

Undertake the divination that you feel is most suited to your present
needs.

Let Tarot transform you. Let Tarot initiate you.

PART TWO

THE SERPENT
OF WISDOM

The Serpent of Wisdom is a meditation in twenty-two parts. It can be adapted for personal or group use. The text can be used in its separate parts or as whole.

It should be used to complement and consolidate the work offered in Part I. Its value will be lessened if it is used too early in a study programme.

The text may be used as a dynamic meditation. It has been used with success in a workshop situation. The meditations are well suited to a dramatic setting.

The order is also flexible. Individual meditations might be combined with Qabalistic study.

The Serpent of Wisdom is offered in the true Spirit of the Tarot which is the Journey of the Wise.

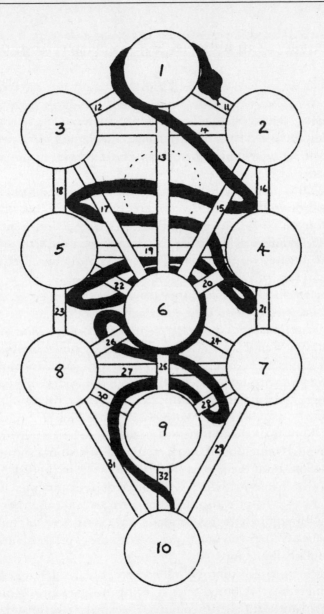

Fig. 29. The Serpent of Wisdom (from *A Practical Guide to Qabalistic Symbolism* by Gareth Knight)

Let the disciple seize hold of the tail of the serpent of wisdom, and having with firmness grasped it, let him follow it into the deepest centre of the Hall of Wisdom.
The Old Commentary

Tarot Trump XXI – The World

תּ

The Thirty-Second Path is the Administrative Intelligence, and it is so called because it directs and associates the motions of the seven planets directing all of them in their proper course.

I am the World. I am called the Great One of the Night of Time. I am to be found upon the 32nd Path which connects Malkuth, the place of manifestation, to Yesod, the place of inner energies. I connect the Kingdom to the Foundation. I am the first journey on the Path of Ascent. I am the last journey on the Path of Descent. I am known to all, though in truth I am recognized by few.

I am the world of effects and appearances. I am the receptacle of invisible forces and powers. I am the outer garment of form. I am Maya, the veil. I am manifestation. I am to be seen in stars and planets, moons and suns. I am to be found beyond your wildest imaginings in places beyond this galaxy. You see me only partially. I am Earth, Air, Fire and Water in combinations known and unknown. I am four in one and one in four. I am seen through the four Holy Kerubs. See my signs, the four fixed signs of the Zodiac; Leo, Taurus, Scorpio and Aquarius. I am whole and indivisible. My sign is the Tau cross, the cross of the elements, four in one and one in four. Remember too that my sign is to be found at the centre of the Cube of Space, at the level of the human heart in the Palace of Holiness. For the human heart which is the heart of humanity presents the first initiation. If you despise the tasks of everyday life, do not seek the Mysteries of Being held by my brothers and sisters, you will find nothing but discontent. When you are at peace with the world, you are ready to move beyond its limitations.

My sign is Saturn, commonly called Father Time. I bring the restriction and limitation of boundaries. I bring the passage of time which touches all manifestation. My colour is black. My tasks may be thought onerous. I am Saturn. My burdens are undeniably heavy. For the world is the field of karma where all must be played out.

I am the hidden dancer, ever moving, never still. Do not be deceived by the appearance of solidity and permanence. Do you really believe in appearance? That is the veil of illusion. I am never still. All is movement. All is in motion. The dance never ceases.

I am the Fool descended into form. See the laurel wreath, bound with red. Look at the Fool bearing a hat of red and green. Like the Fool I am beyond gender. I am Yin and Yang combined. I hold the twin poles of manifestation, opposites ever in polar relationship.

I am the World. I am the Universe. I am the Ring-Pass-Not. I am part of you as you are part of me. We share Life. We share the world of form and matter. Know me. Recognize me. Dwell upon the mysteries of matter and you will glimpse me. I am the World.

Tarot Trump XX – Judgement

שׁ △

The Thirty-First Path is the Perpetual Intelligence, but why is it so called? Because it regulates the motions of the sun and moon in their proper order, each in an orbit convenient for it.

I am Judgement. I am called Spirit of Primal Fire. I connect Malkuth to Hod. I am to be found upon the 31st Path which joins the appearance of form with the will to form.

My letter is Shin, symbolized by the long lived and hard wearing tooth. This mother letter, a triplet of Yods cannot be mistaken; the activity of the Spirit is mine. I am Fire. I am Spirit. I am the awakening moment of realization. I am the discovery that you will make when you realize the spiritual nature of all things. I am everywhere, at all times and in all places, yet until you awaken to my presence I am wholly absent,

Awaken then, or live as the walking dead, the grey ghost adrift upon the sea, floating aimlessly without direction. Hear the clarion call sounded by the angel. Awaken. Exercise judgement. Turn to face the inner realities. Learn how to employ the mind. Learn how to awaken the powers of the mind. Utilize judgement. Connect the mind in all of its parts. Seek wholeness. Unite spirit and matter. I am ever-present. Make the discovery and be amazed.

I am mistakenly called the Last Judgement. Yet I am in fact the First Judgement. You will meet me as soon as you tread the Path for there can be no progress without the exercise of judgement. I am the first act of self-appraisal, the first act of self-evaluation. When you have looked into yourself how will you act? Will you awaken to change or will you return to slumber. Will you hear the clarion call or will it go unheard by you?

Will you be content to live as an automaton, a part of mass consciousness easily swayed by waves of mindless emotional force and indiscriminate suggestion? Or will you truly set out to seek yourself? Dare you seek yourself? Do you have the courage to awaken? 'Know Yourself', is the clarion call of the Mysteries. This note is perpetually sounded at all times and places. The deaf slumber on quite unaware. They drift from lifetime to lifetime carried on by currents unseen.

If you would awaken, if you would journey in consciousness prepare to enter the searing fire of inner alchemy. There can be no growth without fire which purges and reduces. The outgrown, the outworn and the outmoded are as deadwood which prevent new ideas from coming to birth. If you would truly seek the second birth, prepare to burn away the dross accumulated from past actions and forgotten deeds.

I represent the angelic hierarchy as messengers from another level of mind. Our nature is incomprehensible to the human mind. We too have our part to play in the unfolding of your evolution. I am often seen as Michael, the Archangel of Fire, 'the Strong one of God'. Fire brings light and heat. It is the fire of the hearth, the flame in the darkness. It is the candle and the ritual flame. It is the furnace and the fire within the earth. I bring you the Fire of Being, the conscious knowledge of your own divine spark, your own living flame. Awaken to Spiritual Fire. Awaken to Shin. Awaken. For I am Judgement.

Tarot Trump XIX – The Sun
ר ☉

The Thirtieth Path is the Collective Intelligence and astrologers deduce from it the judgement of the stars and celestial signs, and perfect their science according to the rules of the motions of the stars.

I am the Sun, Lord of the Fire of the World. I am to be found on the 30th Path which connects Hod, the sphere of knowledge with Yesod, the astral pool.

I am the Sun. I have been the focus for worship and devotion for I am the visible sign of Life. I am the Lord of the Fire of the World. Do not think that you and I are separate. Our rhythms are joined. The rules and motions of the stars affect all life.

See how humanity dances and rejoices beneath the Sun. My letter is Resh, the front of the head, unlike my sister, the Moon, who holds sway over the powers represented by the back of the head. I bestow the gifts of mind which give humanity a unique place in evolution. I am Sovereign over the powers represented by the front of the head. Here are younger and more sophisticated mental possibilities. I am the powers of the forebrain, the ability to represent and symbolize, abstract, and communicate. I am the ability to plan ahead, remember the past and envisage the passing of time. I bring foresight, insight and hindsight. How will you use my gifts?

You are not bound by instinct or trapped in the moment. You are free to weigh choices and evaluate outcomes. You are not limited to innate learning. You are free to master what is difficult, to learn what is new, to achieve what your forebears could not. You are not limited to concrete reality. You are free to represent your experience through symbols of your choice; words, shapes, pictures, sounds. You are free to represent your chosen symbols by other symbols. You are free from the constraint of the moments, the tyranny of the immediate, the limitation of an event. You are a sentient human being, self-aware, world-aware.

I am the Collective Intelligence. I uphold the many and diverse forms of knowledge which appear separate but are in fact facets of one knowledge. The powers of the mind permit the formation of fields of knowledge.

Walk my path. Travel from Yesod where desires swirl in a confusion of massed thoughts towards Hod where thoughts are made clear. Arise from the group mind. Seek out yourself. Seek out the bright light of self-consciousness. Seek out your own enlightenment.

I am called the Fire of the World. I am a shared light. I am a shared realization. 'Whoever lives by the light of self-realization lives as part of the world, as a conscious part of the unity. Will you rejoice beneath the bright light of self-consciousness? Will you discover what it is to be fully human? Will you dance beneath the sun and celebrate your own mental powers? I am the Sun, Lord of the Fire of the World.

Tarot Trump XVIII – The Moon
ק ה

> The Twenty-Ninth Path is the Corporeal Intelligence, so called because it forms every body which is formed in all the worlds, and the reproduction of them.

I am the Moon. I am secretly called Ruler of Flux and Reflux and Child of the Sons of the Mighty. I am to be found upon the 29th Path which connects the instinctive powers of Netzach to the physical world of Malkuth.

I am the Moon, ever-changing in a constant cycle of birth and rebirth. My tides are your tides. My appearance and disappearance is mirrored in your waters which rise and fall from beaches and banks like a blue cloak. I am the Moon. My power lies in the group instinct. My white light draws the swarming undifferentiated masses, the life forms which reproduce and die as one being. These lives are attuned to my phases. My fullness is seen in your fullness, when my light is bright, species come together to multiply, living things increase by my gentle light.

Pisces is mine. I am the two fishes who swim together like two crescent moons ever joined. In Pisces there is mystery. The Piscean mind naturally understands how to shift to new and deep levels to plumb the depth of the collective seas, to dive for hidden treasures, to seek out the pearls at the bottom of the ocean. The Piscean mind is sensitive to the subtle currents and invisible tides. The Piscean mind is open to the ever-flowing mysteries of life.

I am called the Ruler of Flux and Reflux. I bear the evolutionary tide which is never still but flows unseen. I have watched countless life forms emerge from deep waters. I have watched life forms rise and fall. What shall become of your life form? Twill watch and wait.

My sign is Qoph, the back of the head. Here is the hind brain, the first extension of the spinal cord which some two hundred million years ago took over the task of regulating specialized body functions. This primitive brain processed physical systems and body movements. It is unable to render the higher mental functions which must await further evolutionary development. See my simple creatures emerging from the pool of life. This life knows only how to survive, reproduce and die. It knows nothing of abstraction. It lives an instinctual and programmed destiny. Time passes and I, the Moon, watch. At some sixty-five million years ago the brain underwent another dramatic development with the appearance of the cortex, the front brain. See my dogs. These warm-blooded mammals have both instinct and intelligence. Time passes and I, the Moon, watch as physical change brings sophisticated mental abilities and powers to yet another life form. See the watch towers. These are the creation of the created. They were fashioned first in the mind as ideas and pictures. They were planned and constructed using measure and decision, foresight and intent. These functions belong to another evolutionary leap which takes them from my kingdom into the hands my brother Sot. My world is the world of instinct and biological response. I am called Corporeal Intelligence. I watch over the evolution of forms. I watch over the path of evolving consciousness. Perhaps another dramatic leap of brain and mind is coming to birth in the Pool of Life and I, the Moon, watch.

Tarot Trump XVII – The Star
ﭏ ♒

The Twenty-Eighth Path is called the Natural Intelligence; by it is completed and perfected the nature of all that exists beneath the sun.

I am the Star, Daughter of the Firmament, Dweller between the Waters. I am to be found upon the 28th Path which connects the astral currents of Yesod to the life ensouling waters of Netzach.

I am Tzaddi, the fish hook cast upon the waters of the future. What will you draw up from the depths? Will you have the patience to cast your hook again and again? If you seek only instant results you will surely be disappointed.

I am Nut or Nuit, naked goddess of the heavens. See how my name resembles a sign already familiar to you ♒, I am called 'Nut, the lady of heaven, the mighty one, the great lady'. I am seen bearing a vase of water. My sign is the sycamore tree where weary souls may rest.

Aquarius is mine. I am the Water Bearer. I am the Age appearing over your horizon. See how my sign reflects itself, 'As Above so Below'. I pour new waters upon the Earth. You have felt my presence already in many ways. New ideas and beliefs, new hopes and ideals have sprung up where every drop has touched the parched ground. Each age responds to a new cosmic vibration. Each age reveals but part of a great Mystery. I am the star of a New Age. I bear the promise of fulfilment. I will translate your being into a new form.

Be aware that my waters offer an intoxicating draught for the unwary. Many will be distracted and unbalanced by power. Know that if you would glimpse my starry nature, you must walk firmly upon the Earth.

I am the star Sirius, the brightest star in your sky. I am Sothis, the dog star, also called Sept. I bring High Wisdom and Deep Mystery. See the ibis bird perched in the tree. Here is Thoth, Lord of Wisdom. If you would be apprenticed in the House of Wisdom, begin by dipping the mind beneath the surface. Be patient in your efforts. Do not give up at your first failure. The baptism of Higher Wisdom awaits all who stand prepared.

See the seven stars dancing about the central Great Star. Each is a level of your own being. Each is a plane of being. Here is the blueprint of your own nature, sevenfold and radiant. Do you live as a sevenfold being? Are you prepared for the gift that I bring?

See me in the night sky and acknowledge the stars within. Prepare yourselves for illumination for I am the Star.

Tarot Trump XVI – The Tower

The Twenty-Seventh Path is the Active or Exciting Intelligence and it is so called because through it every existing being receives its spirit and motion.

I am the Tower, Lord of the Hosts of the Mighty. I am to be found on the 27th Path which binds the mind of Hod with the emotion of Netzach.

I am the Tower of the Self constructed so slavishly from desires, wishes and intentions. I am constructed from thoughts and emotions combined. Yet this edifice is falling at its first contact with spiritual force and it will surely fall. The structure of the personality may be destroyed over and over, tested by fire and rocked by crises of mind and heart. Yet the foundation shall stand even as the edifice falls. When the personality is finally established in alignment with spiritual forces, the Tower will serve as a lightning conductor, earthing spiritual realities in safety. See the Lightning Flash which lifts the Crown from its base and causes tongues of fire to burn within. The Tower is the Tree, the blueprint of Being.

It is a mistake to believe that the spiritual path only leads to pleasant pastures and happy meditations. In the quest for Truth and Reality, that which is not true, that which is not real shall undoubtedly fall. As a blade is tempered with fire, so the personality is tempered through life's tests. However, the student who travels the Path in consciousness, actively asks to be tested by fire. And fire shall surely come.

Mars is mine. I am the purging fire which sears. I am the Active Intelligence. I am the response to your own questing. I am the Exciting Intelligence. All is in continuous motion, all is in a state of excitation, all is continuously remade and renewed. You too shall be renewed. From your downfall you shall be reconstructed, from your loss will come gain. You shall arise from the ashes like a phoenix. Are you ready to face the test of alchemical fire?

Peh is mine. It signifies the mouth, the means of verbal communication. The word enshrines both thought and feeling. How shall you use words? Will you speak thoughtlessly and without feeling? Will your words cut and destroy? Will you indulge in meaningless words devoid of substance? When speech expresses the balanced heart and mind, when words convey both thought and feeling, when Peh is the servant and not the master all will be well in the Tower of Self.

Until then the Tower shall rise and fall many times. This is the challenge you accept when you set out to 'Know Thyself'. Will you look back knowing that the security you seek is only an illusion or will you press on into the furnace which is the Tower Struck by Lightning?

Tarot Trump XV – The Devil

The Twenty-Sixth Path is called the Renewing Intelligence, because the Holy God renews by it all the changing things which are renewed by the creation of the world.

I am the Devil. I am Lord of the Gates of Matter and Child of the Forces of Time. I am to be found on the 26th Path, I connect the mental powers of Hod with the illuminating sun of Tiphareth.

I am all your fears combined and blown up into monstrous proportions. See my horns and goat legs, my bat wings and hideous face. What a devil you have created for yourselves. In truth I am Capricorn. I am Earth, form at its most dense. There is no evil in matter. However you have made a god of earthly things and in doing this you have created a monster.

You are enmeshed in matter, driven by possessions, obsessed with ownership. You are chained to me until you discover freedom for yourself. In truth you are ever free, but it is my delight that you do not recognize it. See how easily you might lift my yoke from your neck but you do not reach up. Instead you have become so rooted in dreams of material power and conquest that you are unable to pierce the veil of glamour that I have cast over you.

I am the Renewing Intelligence. Matter is constantly renewed. Creation is constant, never fixed but ever in motion. You are mesmerized by an illusion. You see yourself only as a physical being and dread the phantom of your own death. You see only the one life and wish to take all that you can. You use others as if they were enemies for you do not know that they are old friends and loved ones. You are lost and rootless for you mistake a sense of belonging with possession. Answers are everywhere but you do not even know the question and I laugh and delight in your folly.

Open the eye and awaken. When you awaken I am commanded to release you. But while you sleepwalk I have many tricks to ensnare you and puff up your pride. I will not name them all for they are legion. I seek out your fear, greed, lust and ignorance. These are my footholds in your being but you give them so willingly. Whenever you believe that you are better than another, I laugh. Whenever you believe that matter is inert, I rejoice. Whenever you assert that you are a separate being, I am filled with pleasure. For these beliefs keep you chained to me. Yet I must tell you that I do not look for you. You look for me and when you have discovered all my little ploys you will tire of my games and will want to move on. Until then for you I am the Devil, Lord of the Gates of Matter.

Tarot Trump XIV – Temperance

◻↗

The Twenty-Fifth Path is the Intelligence of Probation or Temptation and it is so called because it is the primary temptation by which the Creator trieth righteous persons.

I am Temperance. I am also called Daughter of the Reconcilers and The Bringer Forth of Life. I am to be found upon the 25th Path which connects the spiritual reality of Tiphareth to the subconscious realms of Yesod.

Sagittarius is mine. I shoot the arrow directly heavenwards. It deviates neither to the right or to the left but ascends by the shortest and quickest route. Mine is the Path of the Mystic.

See that I stand with one foot in the watery realms of Yesod where all is in constant flux. See the Path behind me leading into the distance toward the rising sun, symbol of Tiphareth, the home of the Higher Self. This is your destination and you shall reach it when you are ready. My path connects the personality with the individuality. Only when the personality has been made ready, may the individuality enter. The house of the self must be prepared to receive the individuality as if it were an honoured guest. If the house is overflowing with ego and crowded with self-centred thoughts, what space remains for an invited guest?

If you look in the distance beyond me, you will glimpse the rising sun, which is your spiritual birthright and inheritance. Here you will find yourself. Do not think that such a prize may be won easily. Here indeed is the fabled treasure guarded by dragons and fearsome monsters. The prize awaits as fears are overcome. The quest makes the seeker worthy of the victory.

To attain this prize, which is your own self, you must cross a Gulf which awaits all. Here is the Dark Night of the Soul when all is despair and desolation. The Heart Centre carries a knot or lock within it. Until you fashion the key from within yourself the gate of the Higher Self will not swing open for you.

Samekh is mine. It is the prop which will support you as you travel. For at times you will be weary of the journey and will seek to halt, resting on your beliefs alone. You will indeed travel alone for no friend can travel with you. I am called Temperance and it is through me that souls are tempered. I am called the Intelligence of Probation or Temptation. You will be tempted in many ways to abandon your intent and aspiration.

Do not fear the falling away of that which seems dear to you, for the soul sets its own pace and names its own time. The path is long but you may tread it at your own speed and face my testing only when you are ready.

I offer initiation into the mystery of the Inner Life. Only you will hear the inner voice which summons you to my kingdom, the realm of your true self. I am truly called Temperance, the Bringer Forth of Life.

Tarot Trump XIII – Death
♩ ♏

The Twenty-Fourth Path is the Imaginative Intelligence and it is so called because it gives a likeness to all the similitudes which are created in like manner similar to its harmonious elegancies.

I am Death. I am the Child of the Great Transformers. Lord of the Gates of Death. I am to be found on the 24th Path. I connect the great Transformation of Tiphareth with the outpouring of Netzach.

Nun is mine. It is the fish which swims in the universal sea. As the fish is unaware of the world beyond the sea, so we are unaware of the world beyond physical life.

The scorpion and the eagle are also mine. These are the dual signs of Scorpio. Here lies my mystery. The one is earthbound, a bringer of death; the other flies high soaring towards the sun. Deep are my mysteries which you fear to know. Yet I am the bestower of the gift of the eagle, liberation.

I am your friend if you only but knew it. We have embraced many times and shall do again. In me all are made equal both the great and the lesser. I am no respecter of earthly power or rank. I meet you all in good time. Fear me not but rather prepare to welcome me at the appointed time. Live fully through discovery and wonder. Drink deeply of life's cup. Show the joy of life to others and you will not find me an adversary. Cross my river at the appointed time. Discover my kingdom. The land beyond the doorway has many marvels. It is my secret that I offer you continuity of existence. See the sun rising between the twin towers. Here is a sign of the new life. See the banner that I bear. Its fivefold flower signifies life. It is another form of the five-pointed star.

Fear me not. I will do you no harm. My power is only to bring transformation and in me you will be transformed. For I will separate the outworn from the indwelling spirit, allowing the one to journey on and the other to return into the earth.

I will separate the corruptible from the incorruptible. I will free you from the garment of the flesh, and it shall be a joy to you to lay it down. I will not harm you. I am the Great Transformer. For I am birth and I am death. Death in your world is as birth into my kingdom. Birth in your world is death in mine. All is transformation. Change perpetual is at the root of all things and change has two faces; that of life and that of death.

If you tread this Path you will meet me before you join my kingdom. In my guise as the Great Transformer I will serve your initiation which brings both death and rebirth. To be born into the Higher Self the personality must yield. Remember in moments of fear and dread that I bear a blessing. All death brings renewal for I am in truth Child of the Great Tranformers

Tarot Trump XII – The Hanged Man

מ▽

The Twenty-Third Path is the Stable Intelligence, and it is so called because it has the virtue of Consistency among all numerations.

I am the Hanged Man. I am the Spirit of the Mighty Waters. I am to be found on the 23rd Path. I connect the mind within Hod to the cosmic forces of Geburah. I connect the personal mind to the transpersonal mind.

Mem is mine. Elemental Water, universal consciousness is attributed to me. Like a reflecting surface, I show forth what is shown to me. I reflect that which is above to that which is below. The human mind has the power to receive inspiration and to reflect such visions in works of true imagination. I am the Spirit of the Mighty Waters which reflect impressions from above into the appearance of form below.

I hang suspended by a single foot upon the tree of living wood. I stand upon my head and observe all around. I have a new perspective. I see things differently. For me reality is reversed. I appear strange and disconcerting from your perspective. Yet see that I am at peace and untroubled. We see the world differently, you and I. You accept appearances, I see beyond appearance. You accept material values and strive to accomplish your goals. I accept spiritual values and strive to reveal them through my living.

My value system is quite upside down from your point of view. We are at odds you and I. All things whether great or small have a new meaning from my viewpoint; cause and effect, lower and higher, inner and outer. All have meaning for me which merely baffles and confuses. Indeed your misunderstanding fuels fear and leads to mockery. Yet I can do no other.

My Path is the path of paradox. Water is mine, yet I am called the Stable Intelligence. I offer stability if you could but recognize it. I offer consistency for I am constant. I offer paradox. Stand on your head. Reverse your values. Glimpse reality of a different order. Are you prepared to hang suspended as your old values crumble? Are you prepared to loose the footing of your once certain foundation? Are you prepared to hang upon the Tree of Life as you wait for Wisdom?

If you follow the Path, you too will find yourself mocked and feared by those whose vision is limited to a single dimension. You too will find that your value system has become quite different from what is taken to be the norm. You too will find yourself taking up a sacrificial role. Your spiritual vision will not permit you to defend yourself. Your spiritual stature will not permit you to do any other.

When that day dawns, you too will hang suspended between the world of matter where you walk and the world of spiritual reality which you inhabit. You too will have to discover how to keep your footing in a world turned upside down.

Tarot Trump XI – Justice
ל ♎

The Twenty-Second Path is the Faithful Intelligence and it is so called because it is by is spiritual virtues are increased, and all the dwellers on earth are nearly under its shadow.

I am Justice. I am Daughter of the Lord of Truth, Ruler of the Balance. I am to be found upon the 22nd Path which connects the katabolic powers of Geburah with the balanced powers of Tiphareth.

Lamed is mine. It is the ox-goad. It is the tool with which the driver keeps the ox to the path.

Libra is mine. My task is the weighing of one with another, the balancing of energies and deeds done and not done. My judgement is impersonal and without favour. I am she who preserves the balance. I am Maat, Lady of the Judgement Hall. I prepare you to face the judgement of Geburah. I am Daughter of the Lords of Truth. How will your deeds weigh against a feather? I am the Ruler of the Balance. Will the deeds of your heart balance the lightness of the feather? Even the Individuality must be weighed.

From me nothing is hid. From me nothing is concealed. I perceive all things as they are. Are you ready to stand before me? All shall be revealed. All shall be known. I am adjustment. I am the wielder of the ox-goad which corrects. I hold the sword which cleaves. I hold the balance which does not lie. I assist the Individuality to face the Spirit. Through me spiritual virtues are increased for I purge all that still hinders and skews your unfoldment. I draw upon the fiery power of Geburah. As the diamond emerges from the hidden heat of the earth, the brilliance of your true nature will only be revealed when you have been tested within my fires.

Serve the light and the light will indwell. Follow the darkness and the darkness will summon you. I wield the upright sword, symbol of truth. I hold it before you and with it I administer the universal law. My judgements are just, they cannot be otherwise. All must stand before me.

I can offer you no ease for all must be accounted for. All is entrusted and you must account for your stewardship. I will ask you what you have done and you will answer in truth. I am Daughter of the Lord of Truth. Know that we will meet at the appointed hour. When we stand face to face you will remember that I am Justice.

Tarot Trump X –
The Wheel Of Fortune
כ 4

The Twenty-First Path is the Intelligence of Conciliation and Reward, and it is so called because it receives the divine influence which flows into it from its benediction upon all and each existence.

I am the Wheel of Fortune, Lord of the Forces of Life. I am to be found on the 21st Path. I connect the stabilizing principles of Chesed with the creative outpouring of Netzach. I combine movement with order.

Kaph is mine, the palm of the hand where your destiny is revealed. I am riches. I am poverty. I am the Wheel. I am the turning of your life. I am the Wheel of Fate which binds you to all that has passed before. I am the equilibrating power of karma which is the adjustment of your deeds and the balancing of your pattern.

I am the Wheel which is never still. See the wheel within the wheel. Here is Rota, the wheel. Here is Tarot. Here is Tora, the law. All is turning. I am the motions of the cycles which is the round of the seasons, the turning of the Zodiac and the march of the ages. I am the in-breath and out-breath of the cosmos. There are greater and lesser wheels to which you are bound and some beyond your imaginings. All about you there is turning. All about you there is motion.

Jupiter is mine. I am the principle of expansion. I am the Lord of the Forces of Life. See the serpent, it is the motive power behind all turning. See the four Holy Kerubs again. Here are the four elements. Here are the four letters of the DNA helix combined and recombined over and over again. Here are the four worlds, Yod, Heh, Vau, Heh. See how the Wheel continues to turn amidst the fourfold pattern. It carries an evolving humanity with it as it turns. Are you ready to put your shoulder to the Wheel and aid its turning or must you still be carried? Many cycles have passed and many are yet to come. Each brings its own lessons. My lessons are those of conciliation and reward. Time equilibrates all. The Wheel ever turns. The past, present and future are one upon my Wheel. You have turned with the Wheel many times and shall do again. How many more times will you turn with the Wheel?

See the Sphinx, the guardian of the Wheel. She too combines the four in one. She sits and waits. She will question you closely at the appointed time. Her riddle awaits you. She has the power to release you from the turning of the Wheel with her sword. Are you ready to be freed from the Wheel or shall your unfinished business draw you back again?

Acknowledge the Wheel. It turns at all levels, Acknowledge the path of your own evolution. Acknowledge me. I am the Wheel, Lord of the Forces of Life.

Tarot Trump IX – The Hermit

׳ ♍

The Twentieth Path is the Intelligence of Will and it is so called because it is the means of preparation of all and each created being and by this intelligence the existence of the Primordial Wisdom becomes known.

I am the Hermit. I am the Magus of the Voice of Light and the Prophet of the Eternal. I am to be found on the 20th Path. I connect the wisdom of Chesed with the transforming beauty of Tiphareth. I am Yod, the creative hand outstretched.

Virgo is mine, for I am virgin born of myself. My consciousness is reborn. I am reborn and made new.

I am a solitary traveller. I walk alone. Few wish to travel where I go. Few have been where I shall go. I am alone yet I am not unaided. For I have my staff upon which I may lean and my lamp to light the way. I put my trust in God who has guided me this far and place my hand in his own. I have naught else.

My beacon light is bright. It shines forth into the darkness lighting my way. It shines out too for others if they should have need of it. I am a way-shower and a light-bearer to those who come after me. Yet still I walk without company. Yet there is also one who is a way-shower and a light-bearer for me too.

I am an ancient. My journey has been long and I am not finished yet. I have seen the ways of the world, the delights and pleasures of men. I have known such joys, I have known the suffering of the world. Yet all that is past as a dream half remembered. I have no need of such things now.

I have the light and there is joy in that. I have my path and there is joy in that too. The journey continues and with every step I approach nearer my goal. I have left behind all the trappings of the world, even the personality has little use now for I have gone beyond the lesser self and that is why few will follow me. Yet I am free to pursue my goal, to seek myself. I tread the mountainous heights and still the path goes on. I do not see the summit, yet I know it is there. I see only the next step before me. I know I must travel on. Loneliness is mine. Yet I knew this would be so at the beginning when I agreed to take this road. I am the lamp-lighter on the way.

If you should desire to tread this lonely path too, I will be there, unknown by you, unseen by you. My beacon will shine out as your light will shine out for those who follow. You and I are travellers. I am the Hermit.

Tarot Trump VIII – Strength

ט ל

The Nineteenth Path is the Intelligence of the Secret of all the activities of the spiritual beings, and it is so called because of the influence diffused by it from the most high and exalted sublime glory.

I am Strength. I am the Daughter of the Flaming Sword, Leader of the Lion. I am to be found on the 19th Path. I connect the katabolic powers of

Geburah with the stabilizing form of Chesed. I am the main girder of the Individuality. I understand the use of both severity and mercy. I am stabilized spiritual Strength.

Teth is mine which is the serpent in all its many windings. This is the great power known as Kundalini which raises the human to the level of the divine. It is also Mahakundalini, the Great Serpent which draws worlds into being. I have seen the serpent at work both above and below. I have absorbed and been changed by the Serpent Power. Like the serpent I have emerged many times from myself.

See the sign of infinity above my head. I share it with my brother the Magician. He wears the serpent girdle. I am one with its power. I am Strength. The spiral form holds many secrets. It is the sign of the serpent. I am the Intelligence of all the Activities of the Spiritual Beings. I have seen the spiral at work. I am privy to its secrets.

Leo is mine. This is the alchemical lion. Here is the green lion of raw nature. Here is the red lion of nature subjected to will. Here is the old lion, a consciousness unified through tests and time. See how I hold the king of the beasts. The lion reminds me of the many tests of the past, the trials of inner strength, of failures and overcomings. I am Strength. Yet my Strength is not physical but spiritual power. I am seen in the prisoner of conscience unbroken by years of confinement. I am seen in a total innocence which has the power to shame oppressors. See that I wear a white robe like my brothers, the Fool and the Magician. Yet my robe is covered neither by red or black. I wear only a garland of flowers about me. It is a celebration of life. My strength lies in Pure Being which can never be defeated.

I am nearing the end of one journey. I see the mountain in the background. I must take stock of all my journeys. I am closer to world of Causes now. I may choose my Path. Shall I take on form again and face the lion once more? Shall I seek out a new and unknown turn of the spiral? I shall continue to journey in eternity for I am blessed by the sign of infinity.

I am Daughter of the Flaming Sword. It is raised to give me admission, not lowered to bar my path. I must decide whether to journey on or return to carry others, for I am Strength.

Tarot Trump – VII – The Chariot

ח ♋

> The Eighteenth Path is called the Intelligence of the House of Influences (by the greatness of whose abundance the influx of good things upon created beings is increased) and from its midst the Arcana and hidden sense are drawn forth, which dwell in its shade and which cling to it from the Cause of all Causes.

I am the Chariot. I am called Child of the Powers of the Waters, Lord of the Triumph of Light. I am to be found on the 18th Path. I connect the form-giving principle of Binah with Geburah, the form destroyer.

The letter Cheth is assigned to me. It signifies the field and its enclosure which is both boundary and protection, like the carapace and the shell. I stand within my enclosure which is the chariot. It is the vehicle of my consciousness, the form in which I dwell. Cancer the crab is mine. I am enclosed within a vehicle like the crab. When I reach the boundaries presented by each vehicle of consciousness, like the crab, I will seek out my next home. In this way I have moved through the denser vehicles of expression. My consciousness is now polarized within the spiritual body. I am called Lord of the Triumph of Light.

I stand within this chariot which is the vehicle of my being. It is balanced four square, stable and yet mobile. It will carry me from moment to moment, life to life. I travel through time from incarnation to incarnation each time rebuilding what I require for now, I never forget what I have learned. It is my domain. All is stable and under my control. All is united through harmony and balanced opposition. This is the vehicle I have created. It is drawn by opposing elements, the dark and the light, linked in harmony and yoked together under the control of higher consciousness.

See that it extends in every direction to include all manifestation. See the starry canopy above my head. I acknowledge the stars and the mysteries of creation which they represent. I understand my place in the cosmic scheme. I am crowned by a star upon the green laurel of my brother the Fool. I wear lunar crescents at my shoulders. The Moon rules the sign of Cancer, the crab. Like those born under the sign of Cancer, I have made myself receptive. I am called Child of the Waters. Like water, I am able to reflect that which is above to that which is below.

I am called the Intelligence of the House of Influences. I bear the high influences from Binah within the Supernal triangle to Geburah which is to be found within the Ethical or Moral Triangle. I connect the path of the Individuality with that of the Spirit. Binah holds the spiritual purpose. Geburah translates purpose into action and provides all checks, balances and karmic adjustment. Thus is Geburah feared and sometimes called Pachad. I am seen as conquering hero upon the path of karmic fire. I am called Lord of the Triumph of Light. Flame has been rendered into Light.

I am the ruler of the kingdom within. I rule from the throne of my own being. I understand my own nature. I perceive my path and realize my destiny. I am still travelling, yet my vehicle enables me to travel as I will. I am free for I work in harmony with the universal laws. I am liberated for I rule my own kingdom, and I am answerable to no-one other than my fully-realized self. I am the Chariot, Lord of the Triumph of Light.

Tarot Trump VI – The Lovers
‎ا ‎Ⅱ

The Seventeenth Path is the Disposing Intelligence which provides Faith to the Righteous and they are clothed with the fire of the Holy Spirit by it and it is called the Foundation of Excellence in the state of higher things.

We are called the Lovers. We are Children of the Voice, Oracle of the Mighty Gods. We are to be found on the 17th Path which connects Binah, the mother with Tiphareth, the son. We are travelling towards the supernal triangle where we shall encounter the Mysteries of the Spirit.

Gemini is ours for we are twins coming together as one. Ours is the mystery of polarity, the eternal coming together of opposites. Yin and Yang, darkness and light, male and female, active, passive, force and form. We opposites seek each other constantly. Opposites alone may create. Some call us Adam and Eve. Some call us Shiva and Shakti. Our names do not matter. We stand for the mysteries of creation itself. We show a primal duality in our natures though we affirm a primal unity. This is the paradox within all creation. Unity and duality exist simultaneously.

See the serpent and the Tree of Life, the Tree of the Knowledge of Good and Evil. Here is Creation which is the greatest mystery. It is beyond understanding, beyond all human knowledge. Silence alone points to the mystery of stars and constellations, moving planets and whirling particles. Silence is the virtue of Binah. We are approaching 'The One about Whom Naught may be Said'.

We are to be found upon an exalted Path travelling in the state of higher things. We speak as Children of the Voice. This is the Voice of the Higher Self, the Holy Guardian Angel. We have accomplished both the Knowledge and the Conversation with the Higher Self on our journey. We are now as one, clothed with the Holy Spirit. The Higher Self rules the Kingdom from within.

See the angelic presence, the Oracle of the Mighty Gods. As we approach Binah in the supernal triangle, we are indeed approaching the Mighty Ones. See, the Feminine mode which is actively receptive, responds to the Presence of the Voice. The Masculine can only respond by relating through another mode. At levels of exalted consciousness, the rational mind must give way to the intuitive mind.

Zain is ours. It is the sword whose sharp blade slices away all that is superfluous. Even an angel may wield a sword. The sword divides and separates as Tiphareth is divided from the higher states by a veil, a divide. So we must walk the sword bridge if we wish to continue. Here Faith alone will steady us. The once easy and broad Path has become a test once again. We may say little until you too cross the sword bridge and join us. Then we will welcome you. We are the Lovers, Oracle of the Mighty Gods.

Tarot Trump V – The Hierophant
אח

The Sixteenth Path is the Triumphal or Eternal Intelligence, so called because it is the pleasure of the Glory, beyond which is not other Glory like to it, and it is called also the Paradise prepared for the Righteous.

I am the Hierophant. I am the Magus of the Eternal. I am to be found upon the 16th Path which connects the wisdom of Chokmah with the stabilizing principle of Chesed.

My sign is Vau, the nail which joins two things together as a bridge connects two banks of a river. I connect the outer form of religion with its inner reality. I connect belief with experience. If you wish to rest at the outer appearance of dogma and creed you will glimpse me in all religious forms. If you wish to pass beyond my twin pillars I shall accompany you and lead the way. Look closely at my columns. See the decoration. Here are the pillars of life and death. I transcend even these polarities. For within my Mysteries dualities cease.

I am a living link which joins one generation to another. For I hold the keys to the Ancient Wisdom. The Mysteries never die. The Mysteries are eternal. I am the High Priest of the Mysteries. I stand alone in the inner sanctuary as do all who seek to travel even beyond the levels of their own Individuality. You will find me seated at the gateway to the Supreme Mysteries. I am to be found at the gateway to Wisdom. I connect the Wisdom above to the Wisdom below. I bear the triple crown and carry a triple sceptre. I remind you that you are nearing the supernal realms.

Taurus is mine, the sign of the Bull and the fixed earth. I mediate my knowledge into a form that is accessible to you. My Mysteries connect heaven and earth. I show a great glory, yet having seen it, you must live fully in your earth life. This is the test for all who knock at the door of initiation. You must become the living bridge. As Vau connects, you must equally hold the above and the below, the inner and the outer.

I am the Hierophant. I am the Revealer of the Mysteries. I am the Revealer of Secret Things. My secrets are never told. My Mysteries are beyond words. Yet I will share them with you when you are ready to enter the experience that I offer. I offer you my blessing. Like the Hierophant at the Eleusinian Mysteries we offer transcendent experience. Our function is the same; to directly initiate. I will initiate you into the Mysteries which I uphold and serve. I will be there at your moment of realization. My Path is called Triumphal. Your realization is our shared triumph. The Triumphal Intelligence is the Eternal Intelligence. I am the Magus of the Eternal.

The function of hearing is assigned to me. This is the inner hearing which comes only from the quiet mind and the opening of the higher centres of being. I am always close at hand. Yet how often do you hear my voice? Will you listen in the same spirit as those who approach me in robes of lilies and roses? Hear my voice and I will teach you. I am the Revealer of Secret Things and I will reveal them to you. I offer you the keys that you seek. Are you ready to accept them? I am the Hierophant, Magus of the Eternal.

Tarot Trump IV – The Emperor

ה ♈

The Fifteenth Path is the Constituting Intelligence, so called
because it constitutes the substance of creation in pure darkness, and
men have spoken of the contemplations: it is that darkness spoken
of in Scripture.

I am the Emperor. I am called Son of the Morning, Chief among
the Mighty. I am to be found upon the 15th Path which connects the
dynamic forces of Chokmah with the solar presence of Tiphareth.

I carry the orb and sceptre as symbols of my sovereignty. I am
enthroned upon the great stone seat ornamented with rams' heads.
Aries, cardinal fire is assigned to my nature. I am the dynamic Yang. I am
activity. I am the ram. Remember Knum, the ram-headed, creator god.
Mars, ruler of Aries is mine. Remember the glyph for Mars, the circle
surmounted by the penetrating arrow. Spirit is being subsumed within
matter. Yet I carry the T-cross of Saturn surmounted by the circle.
Ultimately, spirit surmounts matter.

I wear the armour of a warrior king. Metal-working derives from the
fiery furnace and the application of recognized laws. My presence establishes certain fundamental laws. I am the solar principle, active, unchanging. I am constant. See how the presence of the sun establishes basic
relationships for other planetary bodies. Light and dark, heat and cold,
time and distance arise from our mutual relationship. I am the Constituting Intelligence. Through me basic laws come into being. I establish
cosmic order.

My sign is Heh. It signifies a window. It is a single letter assigned the
function of Sight. A window permits both light and vision. I am the
window through which the uncontained dynamism of Chokmah is
filtered into the fiery power of Aries and the strong presence of Mars. I
establish cosmic law. I establish the framework which supports the structure as a window rests in frame. Remember I am called the Constituting
Intelligence. I constitute the substance of creation in pure darkness. I
establish the means of light in that darkness.

It is my task to define and set in motion those basic laws which others
will elaborate. My laws establish parameters. My principles govern possibilities. Acknowledge paradox within manifestation; constancy and
change, stability and motion, limitation and possibility. Cosmic laws

underpin all. Science is mine. I determine the laws. You are free to discover and implement these principles. Unlimited application follows clear understanding.

I am the ruler of a vast kingdom. I am glimpsed in all good rulers but never in tyrants and despots who have failed to understand the right use of power. I am the law but I have no need to exert power. My power lies in the principles which structure and create, build and transform. I am seen in all lawgivers and also in those who use the enquiring mind to discover and understand the hidden laws behind manifestation.

I am a hidden king, Chief among the Mighty. I am an aged king, a reflection of the Ancient of Days, the prime source of all laws. I am the Emperor.

Tarot Trump III – The Empress
ר ♀

The Fourteenth Path is the Illuminating Intelligence and it is so called because it is that Chasmal which is the founder of the concealed and fundamental ideas of holiness and of their stages of preparation.

I am the Empress. I am the Daughter of the Mighty Ones. I am to be found upon the 14th Path which connects the outpouring force of Chokmah with the receiving form of Binah. I am to be found upon the Path which connects the supernal Father and Mother. These are the Mighty Ones. My path completes the supernal triangle, the archetypal triangle which is mirrored at lower levels of manifestation. I am enthroned in my own kingdom, the natural world. I raise the sceptre to denote my sovereignty here.

My sign is Daleth. It signifies the polarity of Wisdom and Folly. The world of form gives rise to both. When appearance is understood, Wisdom results. When appearance is misunderstood only Folly can result. I am called the Illuminating Intelligence. I am the luminous garment of the indwelling light. I am Maya, the Veil. Will you choose Wisdom, or will you choose Folly? What do you understand of my nature?

My sign is Daleth, the doorway. I am the doorway of form through which all things must pass as the Spirit takes shape and manifests in the world of matter. I am seen in the Great Mother. See the corn growing at my feet. Do not forget that it is sacred to Demeter the Earth mother, Though I am the Great Mother, I am the mother of all Great Mothers. I am the portal through which life eternal and unbounded enters the realm of the temporal and limited. I am the form-giving aspect of the divine nature. I am the mother of all creation from where all living things spring. I am within every birth whether of child or star.

I am Venus. See my heart-shaped shield. The circle of spirit surmounts the cross of matter. Spirit and matter are conjoined. I show a face of the Divine Feminine. I am part of the Divine Mystery. You see me upon lower arcs of my being. You know me in part. I am Love. I uphold the primal polarity of opposites without which there would be unending continuity.

I am the primal Yin. I am the dark to the light, I am the negative to the positive. I am the container to the energy. I am the Divine Feminine. Our polarity permits a new possibility, an original creation. See that I am with child. My robe is decorated with pomegranates. I am to be found at all births, the union of Opposites creates new life. Even the molecule and the atom manifest polarity. There are great mysteries in matter. Do not confine your thinking to the earth or even this solar system. Expand your thoughts. Dwell upon the creation of distant worlds and star clusters. I am to be found here too. See my starry crown. I am of the cosmos, of the past and of the future.

You may recognize me as the Great Mother, Mother of life known to you. You may see Mother Nature in my face. You may see the Great Gaia in my being. I am all of these and much more besides. If you revere the Great Mother, if you respect Mother Nature, if you seek to serve Gaia, then you have glimpsed my being and understood my gifts to you. Revere my domain. Treasure my gifts. Acknowledge my presence and you will be rewarded. You and I are one. Your existence manifests through the world of form. Revitalize me with your thoughts, nourish me with your energies, feed me with your caring. We are united. My desolation is your ruin and my delight is your reward. I am the Empress.

Tarot Trump II – The High Priestess
נ ג

> The Thirteenth Path is named the Uniting Intelligence, and it is
> so called because it is itself the Essence of Glory, it is the
> Consummation of Truth of individual spiritual things.

I am the High Priestess. I am also known as the Priestess of the Silver
Star. I am to be found upon the 13th Path between the outflow of Kether
with the transforming power of Tiphareth. I am enthroned on the path
which crosses the Abyss.

I sit between the two pillars of the Temple, Boaz and Jachin, the Pillar
of Mercy and the Pillar of Severity. I sit between them. I am assigned the
Uniting Intelligence. I am to be found upon the Pillar of Equilibrium.
See the equal-armed cross at my breast. Here are the four in one and
one in four. See the stylized lotus petals at the top of the columns. Here is a
symbol of immortality worn as sacred decoration by the priestesses in
Egypt.

See the veil at my back. It conceals Daath, the hidden Sephirah. Peep
beyond the veil and you will glimpse the waters of the cosmic seas,
signifying interstellar space. My realm is cosmic. I am to be found seated at
the portal between the worlds. I am called She of the Silver Star. I wear the
crown of Isis whose star is Sirius, the white star.

My sign is Gimel, the camel which brings the traveller safe through
desert wastes. You cannot travel easily in my realms. You will need to
create a suitable vehicle, for my journeys are exalted and unearthly.
Gimel too is another double letter, signifying the polarity; Peace and
War. In me all polarities are united.

The Moon is mine. I am the High Priestess and I have always served
the lunar current and all its subtle mysteries. I wear the lunar crown. See
the moon at my feet. See that my robe resembles the waters.

I represent the Goddess Isis and her kingdom. I bring her ways to you.
It is my joy to serve her and make her ways manifest. I am a channel for
the Goddess to reveal herself. I am the living representative of the Feminine. I am Wisdom and Compassion. See the pomegranates rich with
seeds. Here is a sign of the Divine Feminine Presence.

I serve the Ancient Wisdom. See I hold the Tora scroll, the scroll of
the Law which is also Taro, the Laws of the Universal Life. These deep
secrets are in my keeping. I am the intuitive life, I cannot explain my

secrets through words but I can share them with you through experience. Are you ready to travel with me? I am the High Priestess.

Tarot Trump I – The Magician
ב ☿

The Twelfth Path is the Intelligence of Transparency because it is that species of Magnificence called the Chazchazit, the place where issues the vision of those seeing apparitions.

I am the Magician. I am also called the Magus of Power. I am to be found upon the 12th Path which connects outpouring of Kether to the form-giver Binah. My number is One.

My sign is Beth, meaning a house. I am the dwelling place of deity. I seek form and appearance with which to clothe the light within.

Mercury is mine. Its colour is yellow which signifies the powers of Air and the Mind. I am the Magician. I set out to discover the real meaning of mind. I apply what I learn in the world. I seek 'Knowledge in order to Serve'.

I am the Magus of Power. See I stand poised beside a Table of the Elements. I seek knowledge. I seek understanding. I seek wisdom. See my table, the microcosm of the macrocosm. All is represented here. In the sword, rod, cup and pantacle I see the four directions, east, south, west and north and the four elements earth, air, fire and water. I see the four tides of the year, the four tides of the day. I see four divine presences and much more. All is represented here on my table, 'As Above so Below'.

I serve the Ancient Wisdom which is timeless and without change. Its truths are universal and pertain to one and all. Its knowledge serves one and all. I seek knowledge that I may serve. I seek the path of Wisdom, the sacred science, the hidden way.

Like my brother the Fool, I wear the inner garment of purity and spiritual reality. Yet I also wear the red robe of life, for in seeking form I will find incarnation. I will descend to the plane of physicality and action. Yet I will not forget my true nature. In my work I will bridge the worlds. I will stand as a lightning conductor between the planes. See how I stand. One hand points upwards towards the source of all spiritual power, the other points down towards the world of manifestation. I will remember how to become a living channel. I will become a mediator of the divine presence when I stand at the table of the elements, the altar of life. The Intelligence of Transparency is assigned to me for I may only serve as a channel when I have become transparent to the Light.

I am crowned with a band of gold for I have awakened the powers of the mind and placed them at the service of my work. I too hold the rod which reminds me that I have chosen to use my will in the service of my work. The sign of infinity is seen above my head. My work has neither beginning nor end. It is continuous.

I wear the serpent girdle around my waist. Its nature reminds me that my work brings renewal. The serpent holds its tail in its mouth. I am reminded of my vows, 'to Dare, to Know, to Will and to be Silent'. I am the Magician, the Magus of Power.

Tarot Trump 0 – The Fool

א △

The Eleventh Path is the Scintillating Intelligence because it is the essence of that curtain which is placed close to the order of the disposition, and this is a special dignity given to it that it may be able to stand before the Face of the Cause of Causes.

I am the Fool. I am also called the Spirit of Aethyr. I am to be found upon the 11th Path which connects Kether, the fountain head to the organizing power of Chokmah. I stand with my back to the white sun, which is also called the White Head. I face towards the future, towards all the possibilities of manifestation. I face towards my journey of descent. I am poised upon the mountain top. I stand above the abyss. My next step shall carry me forwards and downwards. My descent into matter will begin.

I am to be found in all beginnings. The first sign is mine. I am Aleph. My number is 0, the No-Thing from which all things shall come. My zero does not signify a vacuum but a potentiality which cannot be limited by word, thought or number. My zero signifies the Absolute, incomprehensible, beyond all description.

I step from the Void, the source of all that will be. I am the bringer of beginnings, the first born of the cyclic, the herald to the appearance of form. I am Spirit manifesting, stepping out from the mountain top. I am the First Principle, the Spirit of Aethyr which lies at the heart of all things.

I am Ruach, the cosmic breath which animates all life. I am likened to the air, invisible, ever present, life giving. My colour is yellow, the colour attributed to the powers of Air. I am assigned the Fiery or Scintillating Intelligence. I cannot be known by you, though you see me in the guise of universal laws.

I am the first step upon the journey of experience. As yet I am without experience for I have no knowledge of the worlds to come. I journey joyfully for life springs up at my every step. I am Aleph, the ox which turns the first furrow. I am Spirit.

I am the Fool. I journey without experience. I am without guile. I am innocence. My folly is wisdom. I carry all that I need. My wallet is suspended from a rod carried over my shoulder. This rod shall be associated with the powers of Fire and the presence of Spirit. The wallet bears the sign of the eagle. Here is Scorpio whose dual signs of scorpion and eagle point to the deep mysteries of Life and Death. The earthbound scorpion and the soaring eagle embody two opposing perspectives. Which one will you choose?

I am neither male nor female. I am the Fool. I am One. I am whole. I am as yet undivided. See my robe. I bear the white inner robe of purity, already concealed by the outer garment. See the signs that I bear as I journey. Look upon the ten wheels of yellow, each divided into eight segments. Each wheel is an emanation, a Sephirah still to come as my journey unfolds. Each wheel is surrounded by trefoils of green, the colour assigned to Venus, the goddess of love and beauty. At my heart I bear a triple flame within a yellow circle. Remember I am the bearer of the Fiery Intelligence. See also that close to the hem of my robe, I bear the sacred sign of Shin, elemental fire, Spirit itself. I am the Spirit in descent. I bear a crown of laurel with a feather of red. You will see my colours again in another form.

Seek me everywhere for I am everywhere. Look for me in matter, in shapes and forms unlimited, in life forms and currents unimaginable, in possibilities as yet dormant, in futures not yet manifest. Know me as the Spirit of Aethyr. I am the first and the last.

Appendix 1

It was Crowley who counterchanged the Emperor and the Star. According to his own account which is recorded in the Book of Thoth it came about in the following way.

> Frater Perdurabo had made a very profound study of the Tarot since his initiation to the order on the 18th November 1898; for three months later he had attained the grade of Practicus, as such he became entitled to know the Secret Attribution. He constantly studied this and the accompanying explanatory manuscripts. He checked up on all these attributes of the numbers to the forms of nature and found nothing incongruous. But when 8th April 1904 he was writing down the book of the law from the dictation of the messenger of the Secret Chiefs, he seems to have put a mental question suggested by the words in Chapter 1, verse 57: the law of the Fortress, and the great mystery of the House of God. ('The House of God' is one name of the Tarot Trump numbered XVI) to this effect: 'Have I got these attributions right?' For there came an interpolated answer, 'All these old letters of my book are aright but Tzaddi is not the Star. This also is secret, my prophet shall reveal it to the wise.'
>
> This was exceedingly annoying; if Tzaddi is not 'The Star', what was? And what was Tzaddi. He tried for years to counterchange this card, 'The Star' which is numbered XVII, with some other. He had no success. It was many years later that the solution came to him. Tzaddi is 'The Emperor', and therefore the positions of XVII and IV must be interchanged. This attribution is very satisfactory.

Gareth Knight and Dolores Ashcroft-Nowicki follow Crowley's lead and attribute the Emperor to the 28th Path. Robert Wang and Paul Foster Case on the other hand attribute The Star to this path. My own preference is also for the Star. Here is an issue where the student has to come to a personal decision.

Appendix 2

Tarot
Divination and Initiation

The Tarot has become the most popular form of Western divination, yet the Tarot has a deeper and more significant function as a vehicle for initiation. This perspective lifts the function of Tarot from one of providing a psychic mirror to one of providing a series of spiritual keys. As a psychic mirror, the Tarot provides a rich tapestry of images with which to feed the intuition to weave guidance, advice and insight. However, as a spiritual key, the Tarot provides an inner grail with which to weave the wisdom dance of transformation and awakening. Tarot is most commonly defined as a tool of divination and most often forgotten as an initiating journey; the lesser function has come to predominate while the greater function has been overshadowed.

During this period of spiritual resurgence, it is no surprise that Tarot has gained such popularity as a means of divination; Tarot reading has become a new genre within the wider context of New Age spirituality. Without undervaluing its value as a psychic mirror, the transaction between reader and client is an essentially commercial interchange where power lies in the hands of the reader. Even at the close of the most insightful readings, there can be no tangible shift of power, and the reader as the expert retains power, while the client is not empowered through the process. By contrast, the initiating function of Tarot is in the hands of the individual and its greater meaning is to be found not in second-guessing the future but in recognising and assimilating the deep patterns of life itself; this is a process of personal discovery that emerges from an internal sacred space; it is an act of commitment not commerce.

Initiation brings an exchange of power between the initiator and the would-be-initiate. Separated from its mundane relation divination, the Tarot brings empowerment, which lies at the heart of the initiatory process.

Discovering this new perspective on Tarot requires an expanded sense of vision; Tarot has become so familiar that in the process of becoming a widespread commodity, it has lost its numinous glow. Tarot packs have become so varied that the power of the symbol has been stripped away and replaced instead by numerous pleasing images. In this profusion, the current Tarot phenomenon stands in complete contrast to the early Tarot decks which appeared from within the magical fraternity of the Hermetic Order of the Golden Dawn. The Rider-Waite deck has retained a wide popularity despite being designed specifically for members of a closed magical fraternity.

Waite's writings encompass both the divinatory and initiatory functions of Tarot. In The Pictorial Key to the Tarot he states that, 'The Tarot embodies symbolical presentations of universal ideas, behind which lie all the implicits of the human mind, and it is in this sense that they contain secret doctrine, which is the realization by the few of truths imbedded in the consciousness of all, though they have not passed into express recognition by ordinary men.'

Here are the keys to the initiating function of Tarot. Firstly, it is a presentation of universal ideas rendered into a symbolic form. Secondly, this universal philosophy embraces all the experiences known to the human mind. Thirdly, this eternal pattern may be described as a 'secret doctrine', an inner and ever-present picture of the deep life-powers. This understanding arises from personal realization and cannot be conveyed except through inner revelation. The word 'secret' is often misunderstood in its spiritual context; there is nothing that can be whispered from one person to another. Instead the 'secret doctrine' reveals its meaning only slowly and inwardly, and this might be likened to the process of secretion through which substances are produced from a cell, gland, or organ to fulfil a particular function; the process commences inwardly before it culminates outwardly. Finally although these truths are imbedded in the consciousness of all, they are only revealed, that is inwardly secreted, to those committed to the processes of the initiating journey.

Another member of the order Aleister Crowley created the Thoth Tarot with its accompanying Book of Thoth. This groundbreaking Tarot connected the spiritual resurgence of the twentieth century with the mystical and magical practices of Ancient Egypt under the tutelage of Thoth. The Egyptian deity Djehuty–Thoth was later to reformulate as the Greek winged messenger of the gods, Hermes, and became the spiritual template for the Hermetic Wisdom. Crowley's bold and insightful realisation created a powerful and unique initiating system while also retaining Tarot as a method of divination. The Hermetic Order of the Golden Dawn also produced its own Tarot based on the notebooks of Kenneth MacKenzie who visited Eliphas Levi in Paris. It was here in The Golden Dawn that the structure of the Tarot became aligned with the Hebrew alphabet, the pathways on the Tree of Life and astrology thereby creating a complex and multi-levelled initiatory system; Tarot was used both in magical workings, as part of the initiating process, and also as a tool of divination in elaborate new spreads. The Tarot images were drawn by Moina Mathers and each member of the order was required to make a hand drawn copy to be coloured according to the GD's strict instructions.

These three decks emerged from a magical fraternity which recognised and applied both the lesser and greater functions of the Tarot. These seminal packs have spawned a generation of Tarot offspring. But the newest and latest Tarot images have often become detached from any magical lineage. The first Tarot packs arose as intrinsic components of an initiatory path of spiritual awakening. Now however the divinatory function has been popularised and the initiatory function has been eclipsed. The popular rise of Tarot has been a mixed blessing. Tarot cards were until relatively recently associated in the common mind with dubious and dangerous occult practice. This entirely mistaken view has thankfully faded, but it has been replaced by a somewhat sanitised perception: going to a Tarot reader is now on par with a visit to the aromatherapist or any other New Age practitioner; Tarot now has now become safe and acceptable. Though this particular shift in opinion has much to commend it, something has also been lost in the process. Tarot is not the diabolic occult tool that it was once believed to be, but the Tarot IS still an occult tool. The term Tarot has been rehabilitated, but the term 'occult' largely has not and it still carries negative connotations. Yet it simply means 'that which is hidden'; this discarded word still has some insight to offer since it points towards a concealed reality. It suggests a domain that is not immediately evident to the decoding skills of the five senses. Moreover seeking that which is hidden requires a sustained quest and quite possibly demands the development of senses and skills beyond the ordinary. Previous and more confined mindsets defined all attempts to investigate the workings of nature and the human mind as intrusive invasions into God's own domain. Yet in some quarters these still remain the hidden and forbidden realms. So the Tarot is a tool with which to navigate into the hidden realms of the unconscious and with which to create links to the domain of higher consciousness. This is its initiatory function. Divination has no role to play here.

How is it possible for a series of images to effect a reconstruction of being? Each of the early originators of Tarot decks knew the difference between a symbol and an image. This is a fine distinction which has become blurred in the pursuit of artistic and aesthetic display. Only the symbol retains the power to effect transformation; only the symbol has the power to effect initiation. However, without an active process of engagement and ingestion, the symbol remains inactive and cannot yield its transformative potential. The initiatory function cannot become operative until an active relationship is established between the individual and the initiating material. This relationship demands engagement through meditation, reflection and contemplation; these inward processes enable the symbolic images to become absorbed and digested within the psyche as spiritual nutrition. It is this potency which rightly endowed Tarot with its early mystique; consequently, learning the Tarot was once accompanied by vows of secrecy.

The divinatory function can operate wherever two people and a Tarot deck choose to gather, but the initiatory function can only operate within the greater context of a shared spiritual journey. The divinatory function is but a brief encounter with the forces of the Tarot, but the initiatory function is a lifelong adventure into the Ageless Wisdom. This is the gift that the Tarot offers. However the spiritual journey rarely takes place without a map of the territory, for previous travellers have already pioneered the way. Buddhism offers the Wheel of Life, the West offers the Tree of Life.

Appendix 3

Tarot in the Mysteries -
A Path of Self-Initiation

*A talk delivered at The London
Tarot Conference 15th October 2005
at The College of Psychic Studies*

When I began to prepare for today, the enormity and even the folly of my self-appointed title rose in my mind like a great iceberg. The words are innocent enough, 'Tarot', 'Mysteries', 'Path', 'Self-Initiation', but the meaning, depth and import that lie hidden within each word is by analogy just like the iceberg, visible upon the surface, hidden in the depths.

I have spent some thirty years exploring, travelling and interacting in this realm, and since it is truly the place of the Never-Ending Story, my travels go on. So perhaps the best that I can hope for, in the time available, is merely to point out that the iceberg exists, that the Tarot, the Mysteries, the Path, and Self-Initiation have fused into a single entity, that the sacred mysteries of being and becoming can be entered through the visual symbolism of the Tarot, and that you have, in your capacity as a multi-levelled, multi-faceted spiritual being, the power to facilitate this inner process of transformation.

If you have come to the Tarot Conference quite rightly wanting to learn more about the Tarot, to be a more effective Tarot reader - perfectly reasonable goals for the day - then right here at the start, I am asking you to shift the goal posts. I have enjoyed a thirty-year love affair with Tarot, but I only rarely 'read' the cards. In truth, I have little interest in divination, which is I know a shocking confession. If you have an interest in divination, and I hope that you have, then I merely want to build on that interest by exploring another possibility with you, namely the function of initiation.

To initiate simply means to 'begin', and there can be no beginning without proceeding and there can be no proceeding without a pathway. It is common to refer to the Tarot as The Journey of the Fool, the first of the Trumps or Triumphs. However the Path of Self-Initiation does not begin with the image of the Fool but with the image of The World, the last of the Major Arcana, and proceeds forwards by progressing through the Trumps in reverse order from 21 – 0. This is the Path of the Serpent of Wisdom on the Tree of Life.

The serpent, itself a symbol of rebirth, touches each of the 32 Paths, the 10 Sephiroth and the 22 stages on the Tree of Life. So now just once more, I want to ask you to take another mental leap as I explain that from my perspective it is impossible to contemplate the Tarot without the Tree nor the Tree without the Tarot. I am not alone in this view: Robert Wang writes, 'The interlock of Tarot and Qabalah is so precise that the two systems are mutually explanatory.' For me, the Tarot and the dynamics of the Tree have become indissoluble, and they have fused one into another like coal and flame, to steal a truly Kabbalistic metaphor.

So, before moving on, I am suggesting that the images of the Tarot when used in a specific order and in a specific way become a vital part of an initiatory journey of becoming, that is of self-transformation. When used in conjunction and partnership with the Tree of Life, the images of the Tarot serve as keys to the many chambers of being and becoming on the Path of Wisdom.

The value of the Tree of Life is most easily grasped through analogy, and it has been likened to a map of being. If we may think of it as a map, then it offers the traveller 32 paths. Such pathways cannot be grasped intellectually, but only practically and personally through the process of internalisation and ingestion. The term 'pathworking', which has now seeped into general spiritual vocabulary, strictly refers to the process of 'working the paths' on the Tree of Life in the Mystery

School Tradition. Although the term is now loosely used to describe almost any type of inner meditative journey, the word takes us towards the modus operandi of the Mysteries. Before moving on to this, we need to ask how is it that mere pictures hold power? How can the images of the Tarot precipitate a process of deep personal transformation?

To answer these questions, we need to review and re-evaluate the power of the symbol. The Tree of Life is a map of being and becoming conveyed through symbols. The Tarot is a philosophy described though symbols. Together the Tarot and the Tree of Life enmesh to form a Life-Path, a journey of continuous awakening into the nature of what is, the Microcosm and the Macrocosm, As Above So Below.

Although I am able to see the Tarot and the Tree as a happy marriage, it is important to have a clear understanding of this relationship and its history. The Tree of Life belongs to the Jewish Mystical Tradition, Kabbalah (with a K), and predates the emergence of Tarot by hundreds of years. Rabbinical Kabbalah understands and applies the symbol as an instrument of precise teaching in its own unique and powerful way. A long history of persecution has produced a system of sheer brilliance which hides its teachings from the profane while simultaneously speaking to the initiate. This is effected by conveying spiritual truth through the language of symbol and by the profound use of the Hebrew alphabet as a secret sacred code. Just as we now assign the 22 Tarot Trumps to the 22 Paths of the Tree, so Rabbinical Kabbalah also assigns Hebrew letters and associated symbolism and understandably deems the new Tarot correspondence unwanted, unwelcome and utterly irrelevant. But to quote Dion Fortune, 'I do not say this is the teaching of the ancient Rabbis.' She also said, 'The point of view from which I approach the Holy Qabalah in these pages differs, so far as I know, from that of all other writers on the subject, for to me it is a living stream of spiritual development not a historical curiosity.' In other words DF provided a bold and radical revision by taking Qabalah (with a Q) in a different direction. And if we consider ourselves heirs to the tradition in which she stood, we may follow in her footsteps and find the same path of self-initiation into the Mysteries via the images of the Tarot.

To summarise, Kabbalah (with a K) is a Rabbinical Judaic mystical system. Having quietly sustained and nourished many a soul with mystical contemplation, even this worthy tradition finds itself in an unwanted spotlight: Kabbalah has now produced Hollywood-Kabbalah. But I digress, although this newest offshoot from the Tree of Life does serve to make DF's point, that this is a living spiritual tradition not a traditional dogma to be preserved in aspic. Historically, the Tree of Life has incorporated both Christian and Hermetic elements showing that growth and development remain possible. As Bill Gray rightly and succinctly stated in the last century, 'As we grow the Tree grows. It bears a different variety of fruit in the twentieth century than it did in the fourteenth, but it still fulfils its function of producing sustenance for the insatiable human soul in search of its own meaning. What is more its fruits are literally inexhaustible since they constantly renew themselves with fresh supplies of Inner Energies. The harder we pluck the Tree, the more plentifully comes its amazing fruit.'

Having ascertained that the Tree which contains the Tarot is not a Judaic creation, but a much later esoteric evolution, we are now better placed to understand the function of symbolism since it is clear that that both the Tree of Life and the Tarot speak through the universal language of symbols.

It is commonly said that picture is worth a thousand words. We may think in words, but we also understand through symbols. Words have a precision and narrow application which serve the appropriate context, but a symbol permits mental exploration and expansion as the extended association of ideas permits a new process of association to take place. Moreover the language of symbol is universal and cross cultural, and symbolic images - whether as artefact, icon, statue, adornment, painting or mark - reveal the heart of a people. It was Jung who saw that the symbolic motifs of long-deceased cultures were not dead, but very much alive, even appearing in the dream life of patients. This realisation was a turning point and from it Jung elaborated the theory of the collective unconscious and the archetypes within it. As we become familiar with the language of symbolic forms, we gain an entry point into the collective mind, the great cultural cauldron of humanity. Symbolic imagery breaks down the barriers which divide and opens up the realms which unite. Linear local thinking belongs to the limited rational mind, but shared non-local apprehension grows from the universal root of symbolic expression.

The Tarot is treasury of universal symbols, which when internalised have the potential to effect a transformation of being. Its many references and allusions both direct and indirect open the door to a new mode of thinking. Its vocabulary of mythological figures, divinities and angels, cosmic symbols of sun, moon and star, nature's images of trees, flowers and landscapes, its fabulous beasts and animal symbols, offers up the language of the collective unconscious. Jung recognized this when he wrote, 'It also seems as if the set of pictures in the Tarot cards were distantly descended from the archetypes of transformation.'

Having established the value of the symbol, we can now establish how to work with the symbols that the Tarot offers us. Experience suggests a threefold process. The first stage is primarily an intellectual process: recognizing and tracing historical or cultural references, reading, thinking and effectively analysing the Tarot's symbolic structure. The second stage by contrast is primarily an internal process of non-thinking, recreating images in the mind as centres of meditative reflection, being receptive and open to insight and thereby effectively moving from analysis to synthesis in order to awaken intuition: inner tuition. The third stage, which organically grows from the previous two, is primarily one of knowing. The images have become living gateways, interaction becomes experiential and Tarot figures bestow wisdom and blessings, as the initiatory journey deepens.

Using the Tarot for divination can be successfully effected as the first two phases become consolidated. The initiatory path cannot be followed unless and until the third phase emerges. So where might all this lead? What is the point and purpose of immersing the mind in these symbolic forms? Jung, who knew a thing or two about the psychological impact of the symbol, said that psychic development, by which he meant the growth of the whole being not the development of psychism, 'cannot be accomplished by intention and will alone; it needs the attraction of the symbol.' So the symbol is central to the willed process of personal growth, in Jungian terminology, and to the central theme of life, which is the process of Individuation, becoming yourself. If the Magnum Opus of life is seen as the reconstruction of being, then the symbol is centrally placed in this undertaking. As Jung reminds us, 'The transformation of libido through the symbol is a process that has been going on ever since the beginnings of humanity and continues still.'

Becoming yourself lies at the heart of Psychodynamic psychology; becoming spiritually awakened lies at the heart of the Mysteries. But consciously undertaking the path of becoming demands conscious interaction as the symbols of transformation are plucked and ingested through the process of psychic absorption: The Tree of Life and the Tarot in combination provide a treasury of symbolic images. Here is the fuel for the interior work of transformation which is the modus operandi of the Mysteries.

I would like to convey this general principle through some particular examples and provide a brief overview of the initiating function of the three Trumps or Triumphs: Death, The Devil and The Tower. These particular cards of the Major Arcana are often considered foreboding when they appear in a spread but they each describe essential components in the process of self-initiation.

Firstly, Trump XVI, The Tower - also called the House of God or the Lightning Struck Tower - is assigned to the 27th Path. Since it bridges the two sides or pillars of the Tree, we can instantly recognize that this Path and its presiding symbolism of destruction connects two opposing forces or polarities. What opposing forces are joined here? This path connects the 7th Sephirah, Netzach with the 8th Sephirah, Hod. Put at its most simple, where Hod represents the intellect, Netzach represents the intuition; where Hod represents the concrete mind, Netzach represents the emotions; where Hod represents the sciences, Netzach represents the arts; and where Hod represents the scholarly wisdom of Thoth, Netzach represents the Goddess wisdom of Isis. How may these two opposing principles be reconciled and thereby unified except by destruction and reconstruction, both personal and collective? In other words, personal balance and the process towards integration and wholeness require that the predominantly intellectual left-hand brain type must make way for imagination and the instinctive feelings. Conversely the imaginative, artistic, predominantly right brain type must make way for the strength of intellectual rigour. In either case, the processes of destruction and reconstruction are literally involved. So this path and its presiding Trump represent the meeting and unifying of the intellectual and intuitive power. This might be seen as the horizontal polarity between Hod and Netzach. But the Tower also occupies a vertical polarity in its central position, as the way upwards into the next reaches of the Tree. Put at its simplest, destruction and reconstruction permit that which is superfluous to be burned away so that the self, the House of God, is redefined as a vertical channel, a living vehicle connecting the material and the spiritual. I want to stress the dynamic 'livingness' of all such processes. Initiation is but a small beginning in a continuous path of many beginnings.

Turning our attention now towards perhaps the most feared Trump of all, that of Death (XIII) which is to be found on the 24th Path leading from Netzach to Tiphareth, from the 7th Sephirah Victory to the 6th Sephirah Beauty. Once again, making enormous simplifications for the sake of brevity, Tiphareth is the place of rebirth where the forces of the Higher Self or Individuality become operative. To make space, the personality must give up its raucous claim to be heard; in other words, the ego which seeks always to claim, own and possess must give way non-egoic consciousness focussed on sharing, participating, giving and co-creating. This means that the egoic death which takes place through the 24th Path is to be welcomed not feared, for the lesser is giving way to the greater. One again, I want to stress that these are living processes individually experienced in a multitude of ways in real life.

Finally we can look at the initiating function of Trump XV, The Devil, to be found on the 26th Path between Hod and Tiphareth. In other words, the figure of The Devil sits between you and the possibility of higher consciousness, which lies at the heart of the Initiation at Tiphareth. Since the 26th Path emerges from Hod, we are in the realm of ideas and the mind. As the embodiment of Capricorn, the cardinal earth sign, this Trump represents matter itself, and therefore directly asks us to define our relationship with the material world. Which ideas imprison us within matter? Which ideas free us from matter? When we understand that The Devil is just another illusion, the bright gates of Tiphareth may open to us.

So, if I have served to point you in as new direction, perhaps caused you to pause and reflect, then my job is done. I can, as I said at the outset, merely stand holding a signpost, and it is entirely up to you whether you follow the path towards Tarot and The Tree in the service of The Mysteries.

Glossary

Arcanum Latin meaning, 'mystery' or 'secret'.

Archetype A pre-existent pattern which is present always and everywhere in the psyche.

Binah The third Sephirah, Understanding.

Chesed The fourth Sephirah, Mercy also called Gedulah.

Chokmah The second Sephirah, Wisdom.

Collective unconscious A universal, impersonal consciousness built upon the archetypes.

Demeter Greek deity, the Earth Mother.

Eleusinian Mysteries A Greek festival of initiation.

Geburah The fifth Sephirah, Severity, also called Pachad.

Gematria A system which translates words into number values, and compares words of equivalent value.

Hod The eighth Sephirah, Splendour.

Individuation The process by which a person becomes a psychological individual, whole and complete in themselves, a coming into selfhood.

Initiation The beginning of a new phase of personal growth.

Isis The Egyptian goddess of Wisdom.

Kether The first Sephirah, the Crown.

Mandala A circular symbolic pattern.

Major Arcana The 22 Trumps of the Tarot.

Minor Arcana The 56 cards of the Four Suits.

Malkuth The tenth Sephirah, the Kingdom.

Notaricon A specialized aspect of Gematria.

Netzach The seventh Sephirah, Victory.

Neophyte Noviate or novice, a new member of an esoteric fraternity.

Nuit or **Nut** The Egyptian sky goddess.

Otz Chiim The Tree of Life.

Persephone Demeter's daughter.

Qabalah A mystical tradition and training.

Sepher Yetzirah The Book of Formation or Book of Creation.

Sephirah 'Emanation', Sephiroth in the plural.

Superconscious The source of higher transpersonal imperatives such as altruism love, heroism.

Spiritual Psychosynthesis A wider and higher form of Psychosynthesis for transpersonal growth.

Temura Permutation, a specialized aspect of Gematria involving transposition of letters according to certain rules.

Tiphareth The sixth Sephirah, Beauty.

Tetragrammaton The fourfold Holy Name of God.

Thesmophoria The Greek annual women's festival in honour of Demeter.

Thoth The Egyptian god of Wisdom.

Yesod The ninth Sephirah, Foundation.

Notes

Introduction

1. Kaplan, *The Encyclopedia of Tarot*, p.13.
2. Waite, *Shadows of Life and Thought*, p. 184–5.
3. Unpublished lecture addressed to the 'Tomorrow Club' in 1945 by Lady Harris quoted in Wang, *Qabalistic Tarot*, p. 15.

Chapter 1 – Names and Titles

1. Papus, *Tarot of the Bohemians*, p. 264.

Chapter 2 – Symbols and Images

1. Knight, *A Practical Guide to Qabalistic Symbolism*, p. 227.
2. Budge, *The Gods of the Egyptians*, vol. II, p. 108.

Chapter 3 – Archetypes and Meanings

1. Jung, *The Archetypes and the Collective Unconscious*, p. 4.
2. Assagioli, *Psychosynthesis*, p. 24.
3. Bailey, *Ponder on This*, p. 320.

Chapter 4 – Letters and Numbers

1. *Sepher Yetzirah*, trans., Irving Friedman, p. vii.
2. *Sepher Yetzirah*, trans., Wynn Wescott, p. 7.
3. *Sepher Yetzirah*, Friedman, ch. 2, V. 2.
4. *Sepher Yetzirah*, Westcott, ch. 2, V. 5.
5. *Sepher Yetzirah*, Westcott, p. 7.
6. *Sepher Yetzirah*, Westcott, ch. 5, v. 1.
7. Knight, *Experience of the Inner Worlds*, p. 151.
8. Ibid. 160.
9. Case, *The Tarot*, p.15.
10. 'The God of Abraham: A Mathematician's View' in *Gnosis*, no. 28, Summer 1993.
11. Suares, *The Qabalah Trilogy*, p. 55.

12. Ibid. 57.
13. Case, *The True and Invisible Rosicrucian Order*, p. 165.

Chapter 5 – Doorways and Keys

1. *Archetypes*, p. 49.
2. Jung, *Memories, Dreams and Reflections*, p.205.
3. Ibid. 207.
4. Ibid.
5. Jung, *The Structure and Dynamics of the Psyche*, p. 83.
6. Ibid.
7. Steinbrecher, *The Inner Guide Meditation*, p. 45.
8. Ibid. 3.
9. Ibid. 66–74.

Chapter 6 – Stages and Paths

1. *Sepher Yetzirah*, Westcott, ch. I, v. 5.
2. *Qabalistic Tarot*, p. 4.
3. *Inner Worlds*, p. 237.
4. *Practical Guide*, p. 272.
5. Nowicki, *The Shining Paths*, p. 23.

Chapter 7 – Initiation and Individuation

1. *Psychosynthesis*, p. 6.
2. Ibid. 19.
3. Ibid. 192.
4. Ibid. 193.
5. Ibid. 197.
6. Ibid. 204.
7. *Archetypes*, p. 288.
8. *Memories*, p. 235.
9. Harding, *Women's Mysteries*, p. 209.
10. *Structure and Dynamics*, p. 79.
11. Ibid. 79.

Chapter 8 – Mandalas and Divination

1. *Memories*, p. 220.
2. Ibid. 221.
3. *Archetypes*, p. 366.
4. *Memories*, p. 221.

Bibliography

Ashcoft-Nowicki, Dolores. *The Shining Paths*, Aquarian Press, 1983.
—— *Inner Landscapes*, Aquarian Press, 1989.
Assagioli, R. *Psychosynthesis*, Turnstone Press, 1986.
Bailey, A. *Ponder on This*, Lucis Trust, 1971.
Cannon Reed, Ellen. *The Witches' Qabalah*, Book I, 'The Goddess and the Tree', Llewellyn 1985.
Case, Paul Foster. *The Book of Tokens*, Builders of the Adytum, 1978.
—— *Tarot: A Key to the Wisdom of the Ages*, Macoy Publishing Company, 1947.
—— *The True and Invisible Rosicrucian Order*, Weiser, 1985.
Crowley, A. *The Book of Thoth*, Weiser, 1982.
Denning, Melita and Phillips, Osborne. *Magical States of Consciousness*, Llewellyn, 1985.
Dummett, Michael. *Visconti–Sforza Tarot Cards*, George Braziller Inc., New York, 1986.
Halevi, Z'ev ben Shimon. *Kabbalah*, Thames & Hudson, 1979.
Hoeller, S. *The Royal Road*, Wheaton, 1975.
Jung, C.G. *Memories, Dreams, Reflections*, Fontana, 1963.
—— *The Structure and Dynamics of the Psyche*, Routledge & Kegan Paul, 1977.
—— *The Archetypes and the Collective Unconscious*, Princeton University Press, 1980.
Kaplan, Stuart R. *The Encyclopedia of Tarot*, 3 vols., U.S. Games, 1978/1986.
Knight, Gareth. *Experience of the Inner Worlds*, Helios Books, 1975.
—— *The Treasure House of Images*, Aquarian Press, 1986.
—— *A Practical Guide to Qabalistic Symbolism*, Helios Books, 1980.
Lawlor, Robert. *Sacred Geometry*, Thames & Hudson, 1982.
Papus. *The Tarot of the Bohemians*, Melvin Powers, Wilshire Book Company, 1975.
Pollack, R. *Seventy Eight Degrees of Wisdom*, Vol 1 and 2. Aquarian, 1983.
Sepher Yetzirah. The Book of Formation, trans. by W. Wynn Westcott, Weiser, 1975.

Sepher Yetzirah. The Book of Creation, trans. by Irving Friedman, Weiser, 1977.

Suares, Carlo. *The Qabalah Trilogy*, Shambhala, 1985.

Waite, A.E. *Shadows of Life and Thought*, London, 1938.

Wang, Robert, *The Qabalistic Tarot*, Weiser, 1983.

Williams, Strephon Kaplan, *Jungian Senoi Dreamwork Manual*, Journey Press, Berkeley, 1980.

Williams, Charles. *The Greater Trumps*, London, 1964.

Index